kissing

kissing

everything you ever wanted to know about one of life's sweetest pleasures

ANDRÉA DEMIRJIAN

A PERIGEE BOOK

Most Perigee Books are available at special quantity discounts for bulk purchases for sales promotions, premiums, fund-raising, or educational use. Special books, or book excerpts, can also be created to fit specific needs.

For details, write: Special Markets, The Berkley Publishing Group, 375 Hudson Street, New York, New York 10014.

THE BERKLEY PUBLISHING GROUP
Published by the Penguin Group
Penguin Group (USA) Inc.
375 Hudson Street, New York, New York 10014, USA
Penguin Group (Canada), 90 Eglinton Avenue East, Suite 700, Toronto, Ontario
M4P 2Y3, Canada (a division of Pearson Penguin Canada Inc.)
Penguin Books Ltd., 80 Strand, London WC2R 0RL, England
Penguin Group Ireland, 25 St Stephen's Green, Dublin 2, Ireland (a division of Penguin Books Ltd.)
Penguin Group (Australia), 250 Camberwell Road, Camberwell, Victoria 3124, Australia
(a division of Pearson Australia Group Pty. Ltd.)
Penguin Books India Pvt. Ltd., 11 Community Centre, Panchsheel Park, New Delhi—110 017, India
Penguin Group (NZ), cnr. Airborne and Rosedale Roads, Albany,
Auckland 1310, New Zealand (a division of Pearson New Zealand Ltd.)
Penguin Books (South Africa) (Pty.) Ltd., 24 Sturdee Avenue, Rosebank, Johannesburg 2196, South Africa

Penguin Books Ltd., Registered Offices: 80 Strand, London, WC2R 0RL, England

Copyright © 2006 by Andréa Demirjian
Text design by Stephanie Huntwork
Cover design by Ben Gibson
Cover art by Getty Images

PRINTING HISTORY
Perigee trade paperback edition / January 2006

ISBN: 0-399-53234-X

PERIGEE is a registered trademark of Penguin Group (USA) Inc.
The "P" design is a trademark belonging to Penguin Group (USA) Inc.

This book has been cataloged by the Library of Congress

PRINTED IN THE UNITED STATES OF AMERICA
10   9   8   7   6   5   4   3   2   1

With love to my beautiful grandmothers

Anastasia Alexiou Cotsonas

and

Nevare Donabedian Demirjian

Angels in heaven as on earth.

x ♡ o

Andréa-Nevare

contents

Face to face, he drew her near.
Gently, his lips grazed against her softness.
Moving closer, the sweetness of his
breath made her falter.
Waiting no longer, she kissed him!
—A.D. (CIRCA 1988)

notes from a kissing connoisseur

"Where one drop of blood drains a castle,
so one kiss can bring it alive again."
SLEEPING BEAUTY (DISNEY, 1959)

**K**issing. A wise girl-friend once noted it's a sweet piece of the big love puzzle. And most of us girls, being the super sleuths that we are, have a re-markable ability to spend an inordinate amount of our time considering this intricate and intriguing little mys-tery of the heart. In our pursuit of romantic nirvana, we think about kissing inside and out. Front, back and center. Morning, noon and night. In the shower, on the tread-mill. Driving. Shopping. Doing our makeup. Sleeping. Eating. Whatever and whenever.

When the self-evaluation is semi-digested, we discuss it with our girlfriends. Sharing experiences, looking for meaning, finding relevance in subtle nuances and casual gestures. Making a silk purse out of a sow's ear. It's amazing how our imaginations can spin yarn when it comes to kissing, convincing us of truths that might not otherwise exist.

But beyond the shiverin', twitterin,' toe-twitchin,' sexy-feel-good of it, what do we really know about kissing? Is it truly the doorway to the soul that poets wax on about? The barometer for connubial bliss? The yin to the yang? The moth to the flame?

For me, understanding the meaning of this intoxicating interaction has been my manifest destiny. I've long felt its gravitational pull. It's mesmerized me, preoccupied me and shaped my perception of things.

As a wee one, I remember believing that only married people could kiss on the lips. In my innocence, I sensed there was an intimacy to this sacred act that warranted an official union. How did I account for characters on TV who kissed each other all over? According to a six-year-old's code of ethics, thin pieces of cellophane must have sheathed their mouths, preventing unsanctioned lips from touching. (Clearly I was familiar with Medieval social manifestos on propriety and decorum because kissing was considered serious business back then. Should a girl and boy be caught kissing in public, they could be forced to the altar!)

Eventually I came to appreciate that a blood test and license was not a prerequisite for locking lips. I also came to understand the traffic term *rubbernecking* didn't refer to car bumpers kissing as they inched lazily along a highway.

And I'd also come to know that the quest for kissing of the truly romantic kind would be a tad challenging in "grown-up" life. Despite a spirit that's always been ready, willing and able, my fulfillment would swing from feast to famine. More like a pattern of whirlwind kissing escapades dotted and dashed like Morse code in between desolate stretches of unsolicited abstinence. And often, the hiatuses lasted longer than what would be considered humane by any ethical organization protecting the well-being of defenseless animals from becoming coats, handbags and stylish shoes.

Not long ago, I was experiencing a seemingly terminal kissing pause—the kind that has you appreciating just how a nun can live a life of chastity. When lo and behold, I found myself at a dinner party seated next to a guy with major *kiss-a-risma*. He was chatting up the lady to his left, but his magnetic allure distracted me from my companion to the right.

Somewhere toward the end of the main course we started talking. I liked the way he thought. I liked the way his mouth looked when he talked. I liked the ease that washed over me. If I wasn't such a chicken, I might've placed my hand on his leg under the table.

The evening started to wind down. I offered to share a cab. When he got out, I did, too. I lived nowhere near. But knew it was now or never. Summoning some bravado, I asked, "How 'bout a drink?" We moved from bistro to bistro, sipping wine and sensing that palpable crescendo of chemistry and synchronicity. Somewhere in between deep personal questions like "Have you ever had a broken heart?", the kissing began. It was kissing of the highest order. And a flatlined libido was suddenly shocked back into a healthy rhythm.

The kissing that occurred on what I've since anointed "the great bistro adventure" would break the drawn-out dry spell. Almost overnight, a whistlin' tundra was transformed into a lush, tropical jungle. And as "It's Raining Men (thunderclap), Hallelujah, It's Raining Men (thunderclap) and Men . . ." thumped in my heart, I began an unprecedented kissing romp, jumping from lily pad to lily pad.

Months later, waking up one morning in a hazy state of early-dawn daydreams after an evening of some very scrumptious kissing on a beach under a twinkly black night, I began flipping through the "Boys I've Kissed" pin-up calendar in my mind. Forever possessing a fourteen-year-old mentality, and in a moment that can only be likened to someone "huff-huffing" on their fingers and "buff-buffing" them against their pecs, I pulled myself out from under the cozy covers to scribble all this action down.

These notes of historical (or hysterical) significance got me thinking about the many utterly delightful kissing experiences I've been lucky to have. Naturally, as girls are prone to do, I began to rate the kissing, and relive the sexiness of the exceptionally sensuous ones.

I also began to ponder other kissing questions. How did the ritual of kissing actually begin? What provoked the first lip-to-lip connection? Is the kiss as we know it today similar to the kisses of yesterday? Beyond that, what's the chemistry of kissing? The biology and physiology of it? Its place in history? Is it really the natural, cheaper way to plumper, poutier lips? So many questions!

Until now, my thoughts about this delightful breath-taking activity had pretty much been idle cosmic reflections, not the wherefores and whys. Now I knew I just had to find out.

In answer to these earth-shattering questions, *Kissing* hopes to shed light on a multitude of amazing kissing facts and information. There's lot of interesting *Who knew?* tidbits. Like the Darwinian genesis of kissing in the land of the cavegirls, and how this most pleasurable act evolved over the centuries, how it's enjoyed around the world today, and more.

Kissing also shares the essentials every girl needs to turn her partner into putty: hot tips and sexy techniques. Fun exercises to improve your pucker. Exotic, sensational new kisses to try. Friendly reminders of some do's and don'ts. And other important commandments for satisfying kissing. It even attempts to shed light on what a guy wants from kissing.

I hope after reading the book that your knowledge will be most impressive at cocktail parties, and your kissing skill and finesse sought after at your own exclusive velvet rope "after party."

Throughout *Kissing*, you'll also find results from a survey I conducted with a cross section of women and men. Hear what they think about puckering up as they spill the beans on their kissing thoughts and escapades. Take the survey, too; it's included at the end of the book, along with showing you a way to take a look at your kissing experiences. Fill in the blanks on your own, or with your girlfriends at a bachelorette or pajama party.

Women are often told they'll need to kiss many a frog before their prince. Or that kissing is the key ingredient to a happy romantic life. But there's much more we need know to ensure that we'll enjoy satisfying kissing.

So spread a little love with a kiss. And remember the *Kissing* credo:

Kiss with enthusiasm and respect.
Kiss with abandon and no regret.
Kiss knowing each one counts for something.
And forever be in quest of kissing.

♡

kissing

1
the many faces
of a kiss

"A kiss can be a comma, question mark or an exclamation point. That's basic spelling that every woman ought to know."

MISTINGUETT (FRENCH ACTOR
JEANNE MARIE, BOURGEOIS, 1955)

Kissing. It conjures up a swash of wonderful emotions, sensations and meanings. Originally an instinctual prelude to mating, kissing transformed humankind by becoming the universal glue that binds. A nonverbal communication that declares a thousand things. A bridge to our past, present and future. Destiny where "soul meets soul on lover's lips" (Percy Bysshe Shelley).

A kiss is both given and received. It's spontaneous. Unique. Intuitive. Indelible. Secretive. Affectionate. Passionate. Romantic and blissful. Heavenly and holy. It can be sexual. Or pure. Innocent. Or provocative. It can't be faked. Its duality can bring great joy. Or deep sorrow. Render you weak. Or brave. Vulnerable. Or invincible. It can awaken. Or even kill. A link between our inner psyche and outer world, a kiss is a mysterious, yet revealing, life-sustaining force. A signature of love. And reverence. A symbol of tragedy. And betrayal. Of greeting and farewell. Simple yet so complex, its power is infinite.

Mostly, a kiss is simply a nice way to say hello. And spread a little love. It's also fun to do in a shower, at the movies, on a park bench, over a candlelit dinner or in bed first thing in the morning. There's really no better way to spend time with someone you love, like or unabashedly lust for. Whatever else it may be, kissing is a beautiful thing.

warm 'n fuzzy

At times, kissing is like sipping a tasty, warm, cup of cocoa with teeny floating marshmallows and whipped cream. Lying on a big cozy couch snuggled up lip to lip (and skin to skin) while the rain drizzles softly against the window, you kiss lazily to the song "Besame Mucho" (translation: "Kiss Me a Lot"). You're utterly relaxed. The world outside muffled. Catnaps in between dreamy soft kisses and sweet whispers. An almost Zen state of kiss.

This is the perfect kind of kissing when you're tired, need a little TLK (tender loving kissing!) or just feel like spooning in the romantic intimacy of being so close to someone that you literally share their breath.

quivering shivering

"A kiss could throw shivers throughout her body."
ANAÏS NIN (*DELTA OF VENUS*, 1969)

A kiss can also be a frisky, fun, delectable burst of electricity that literally knocks you to your knees. This is that kiss that outright intoxicates you, diminishes your capacity to think, causes midday distractions that lead to sky-high nighttime fantasies, and hampers your ability to speak clearly and succinctly. It can even reduce you to feeling like an awkward teenager whose unrequited crush on the high school hottie leaves her banging into locker doors during hallway sightings.

I've been known to get loopy and "skip to my lou" when I think of that super-suave secret agent man 007 and certain mortals I've been lucky enough to kiss. There's no special profile. Just that certain *kiss-a-risma* when wrapped the right way that makes them totally irresistible. Whatever it might be, you become fixated. I refer to this mania as the "James Bond." His mere essence could provoke an extreme sacrifice for but one fleeting moment of rapture. I'd literally give my eyeteeth just to gently caress the lower lip of that sexy spy!

purely platonic

"Platonic friendship is the interval between the introductions and the first kiss."

R. WOOD, ED. (*THE MODERN HANDBOOK OF HUMOR*)

On the flip side of the quivering shivering variety, there's the "platonic" kiss. This is nicknamed after that ancient Greek philosopher Plato, who put himself on the map when he opened the "Academy" back in 385 B.C. It's believed when students and scholars entered the Academy, they'd "high-five" each other with a friendly salutation kiss to the cheek, hand or shoulder. Since only men were allowed in, the "platonic" kiss was devoid of any sexy inclinations. And thus why we girls when asked "What's up?" about a boy we're hanging with have casually feigned, "Oh, its just platonic."

sweet as honey

"The mother's first kiss teaches the child love."
GUISEPPE MAZZINI (1805-1872)

Then there's the bonding kiss between a parent and child, or grandparent and grandchild. This exchange is filled with the purest, unconditional love that washes over you like a sweetly fragrant bubble bath. Super delectable, it swells the heart with an unparalleled sense of belonging.

All my grandparents were known for kissing me (and each of their grandchildren) with unusual frequency and gusto. Grabbing my little mug, they'd come into my face for a soft, teeny nibble. I'd flex my cheeks and cry, "Owww, that hurt!" Despite my yelps, and exaggerated wiping of the face, I knew this was a demonstration of their unadulterated love. As I grew, there'd be nothing more delicious than curling up with my grandmas for some love bites. Their sweetness dripped like the honey syrup in their baklavas.

what happens to our bodies when we kiss?

"Kisses are like confidences—one follows the other."

DENIS DIDEROT (1713-1784)

Be it an impulsive peck of affection or a succulent languorous lip-lock, a kiss can tickle like an innocent crush or make you shudder with anticipated delight. No matter what kissing means to you, it's sure to get your juices flowing.

WE'RE WIRED FOR PLEASURE

Experts say all that "warm 'n fuzzy" oozing through us like the raspberry jam piped into a powdered jelly donut, stimulates our brain. When lips and tongues intertwine, our neural networks get fired up. Zing! A signal transmits the 411 from the eensy nerves in our mouths, lips and nose to the brain in a nanosecond. That little cranial box is the ultimate operating system. Our hearts beat double time. Our lungs pump pump pump. Our salivary glands mist like a garden sprinkler. And our jawbones unhinge as our snake-charmed tongues come a' twirlin' out like a swizzled cocktail stirrer (did you know the jaw is the only bone in the skull with an open-and-shut latch?).

> "The anatomical juxtaposition of two obbicularis oris muscles in a state of contraction."
> DR. HENRY GIBBONS, 1808-1884

With tongues and lips slinking and sliding all over, that signal zips along the spine (our internal cable wire). Messages from the pancreas and adrenal glands tap our pelvic nerves. Everything starts puffing and expanding. Arteries and veins burst open wide. Lips swell like they've been stung by bees. With all that blood rushing and spreading through us like a wildfire, we get all flushed. And tingle in certain places. It's like we've been tickled with a feather. Ooo la la, your toes start to sing!

"It is the passion that is in a kiss that gives to it its
sweetness; it is the affection in a kiss that sanctifies it."
CHRISTAIN NESTELL BOVEE (1820-1904)

Getting scientific for a moment, good passionate kissing causes a norepinephrine, dopamine and phenylethylamine rush (also known as PEA). These neurotransmitters collide with the brain's pleasure receptors, creating feelings of delirium. Parachuting, bungee jumping and other extreme sports cause a similar adrenaline surge. If you ask me, that's really a lot of work with the renting of all that equipment and stuff (let alone the risk) for a high you could get in your living room.

did you know ?

Our brains have a function that helps us locate each other's lips in the dark. And since about 92 percent of us keep our eyes closed when kissing, this let's us zero in on our sweetie's lips like a stealth missile!

AN INFORMATION ROUND-UP

Accenting all this delightfulness, kissing is instructional. Just ask a philematologist (one who studies kissing). They'll tell you kissing is an instinctual survival mechanism that allows us to send and receive vital information.

With a kiss, a girl sips a guy's pheremonal cocktail. Brushing against his cheeks and lips, she picks up his scent, his smell and his taste. It can also signal his intentions, expressions and personality. If his hygiene and skin care runs rugged or fair. Whether he's generous or a tad stingy. Even if he's had Chinese for lunch.

With that first kiss, she drinks in his organic tattoo. Her tongue takes a sensuous reconnaissance. The scents and smells speak to her in volumes. But not all discoveries are made in the mouth. Like that thing about the tongue being a metaphor for a boy's "you know what." Now ladies, before your imaginations run wild to a *Sex and the City* "Samanthaism," it's a myth. Like the size of the foot. Just concentrate on the kiss. That's your portal to all-around happiness. Satisfaction. And maybe connubial bliss. Let the rest be a surprise.

one kiss can speak a thousand words

"The decision to kiss for the first time is the most crucial in any love story. It changes the relationship of two people much more strongly than any final surrender; because this kiss already has within it that surrender."

"OF LIFE AND LOVE", EMIL LUDWIG

(1881-1948)

We girls have all talked about how we know from just a kiss whether or not a guy is right for us. Given the primal physiology and destiny of kissing, it's no wonder we're known for saying, "I knew from the moment we kissed . . ." It's the chemistry of that first kiss that determines whether you're on the romantic scenic route, driving away like Barbie in a pink convertible to live happily ever after in a dream house, or back to the frog pond, praying the next web-footed amphibian does a princely morph. Between the power, the magic and the promise of love, sex and even marriage, it can be pretty intense stuff.

> "... then I did the simplest thing in the world. I leaned
> down ... and kissed him. And the world cracked open."
> AGNES DE MILLE (CHOREOGRAPHER AND
> DANCER, 1905-1993)

Even long before magazine subscriptions and cable TV talk shows, many women were living and dying by this "I knew from the moment we kissed" philosophy. Just think about the centuries of sweet and sorrowful expressions by artists, poets and musicians. How many other activities can twist and turn between great hope and crushing despair? It's no wonder the prospect of a first kiss can be a bit intimidating.

> "You may conquer with a sword,
> but you are conquered by a kiss."
> DANIEL HEINSIUS, 1580-1566

> "Let him kiss me with the kisses of his mouth:
> for thy love is better than wine."
> SONG OF SOLOMON (THE BIBLE,
> SONG OF SOLOMON, 1:1-2)

did you know ?

Animals are big kissers, too. Doggies enthusiastically lick their mates. Chimps are major French kissers. They'll slip the tongue not only to their lovers, but mothers, brothers and babies (no wonder they're always screeching with joy!). Elephants slide their trunks inside each other's mouths. Birds bang beaks. Bugs stroke legs and bellies. And turtles rub noses. Even fish kiss. A species called the "kissing gurami" kiss for as long as twenty-five minutes at a time. That's some puckerin'!

"A dog will kiss the hand that has no food to offer."

GEORGE G. VEST ("EULOGY TO THE DOG", 1870)

the definition
of a kiss

"What is a kiss? Why this, as some approve: The sure
sweet cement, glue and lime of love."

ROBERT HERRICK, 1591-1674

KISSING BY THE DICTIONARY

Every dictionary has a slightly different set of definitions
for a kiss. Here's a sampling:

1. To salute with the lips, as a mark of affection,
   reverence, submission, forgiveness, reconcilia-
   tion, parting, etc.
2. To touch gently, as if fondly or caressing.
3. To make or give salutation with the lips in
   token of love, respect, etc.; as, kiss and make friends.
4. To meet; to come in contact; to touch fondly.
5. A small piece of confectionery.

6. A cookie made of egg whites and sugar (a.k.a. a meringue).

That good ol' British bloke Shakespeare called a kiss a "*seal of our love.*" Another well-known poetic Brit named Sammy Coleridge described it as "*nectar breathing.*" All pretty romantic stuff.

> "A kiss is something you cannot give without taking and cannot take without giving."
>
> ANONYMOUS

True to the oddities of the amazing English language, there are multiple ways you can refer to a kiss. Over eighty, to be exact. Try these for a little variety next time you're in the mood, or when you simply want to impress someone with your prolific lingual abilities:

first base	hook up with	neck
tongue wrestle	make out	lock lips
scam	tonsil hockey	get together with
peck	French	mash

canoodle

snogging

deep smooch

smacking

paste

wham

baisemain

orad

wetly

tell

interosculate

exosculate

basial

savor

clap

taste

begrime

coo

dally

grime

pet

spoon

toy

whisper sweet
    nothings

snoggle

buss

soul smooch

osculate

candy smooch

ba

deosculate

dahl

eroo

ido

mouth

pooch

salt

caress

snatch

embrace

besmoil

blow a smooch

dirty

lollygag

smirch

sweet talk

trifle

sugar

fool around

smack

slap

belt

molasses smooch

kess

suaviation

scotch smooch

kith

smatch

tony

pooch out

lip

smatter

salute

bang

bill

copulate

foul

make love

smudge

tarnish

wanton

snog

KISSING SYNONYMS

A thesaurus offers a plethora of ways to describe a good smooch: abandon, accost, address, attouchement, bid good day, bid good morning, blow a kiss, bob, bow, bow to, breath, brush, brush by, buss, caress, come in contact, contact, contingence, curtsy, cutaneous sense, desert, dismiss, disregard, embrace, exchange greetings, feel, feeling, fingertip caress, flick, forsake, give up, glance, graze, greet, greeting, hail, hand-clasp, hand-mindedness, handshake, hello, hit, how-do-you-do, hug, ignore, impinge, impingement, impingence, kiss hands, lambency, lap, lick, lift the hat, light touch, lip, neck, nod, nod to, nudge, osculate, osculation, peck, pull the forelock, relinquish, renounce, repudiate, rub, salutation, salute, say hello, scrape, sense of touch, shake, shake hands, shave, sideswipe, skim, skirt, smack, smacker, smile, smile of recognition, smooch, spoon, squeak by, stroke, sweep, tactile sense, taction, tangency, tap, tentative contact, tentative poke, touch, touch lightly, touch the hat, touch upon, touching, uncover, wave and whisper.

KISSING IDIOMS
AND ACRONYMS

The English language also comes complete with colorful idiomatic expressions:

Kiss of Death
Kiss Off and Kiss It Off
Kiss That One Goodbye
Kiss The Blarney Stone (more on this one later . . .)
Kiss and Tell

And we're all familiar with the K.I.S.S. acronym—Keep It Simple Stupid. The K.I.S.S. rule applies more to business than kissing (one would hope!), e.g., managers who want to keep things simple, easy to use, understand, etc.

Think of K.I.S.S. as kind of a "kissing cousin" to "Less Is More", i.e., fewer candles are more romantic for mood lighting vs. enough to fill a church (that could be a fire hazard!).

What K.I.S.S. should really stand for is how you want to be kissed:

Keep It Sweet Sunshine

Keep It Sexy Sweetie

Keep It Sizzlin' Sexy

Keep It Scandalous Stud

Keep It Savage Sugar

Keep It Saucy Sally

Keep It Sinful Sammy

Keep It Smooth Seymour

Keep It Soaring Superstar

KISSING SLANG

Kiss my grits

Kissing cousins

Sealed with a kiss

Give me some sugar

Sweet sixteen and never been kissed

Stealing a kiss

I kiss the ground you walk on

Kiss me, you fool

Shower with kisses

Of all the definitions and expressions of a kiss, this one is spot on:

"A contraction of the mouth due to an
enlargement of the heart."

ANONYMOUS

what's your
definition of a kiss?

Throughout this book you'll find the responses from my kissing survey. The comments from these ladies of all ages and Ms./Mrs. status are real and candid, and they express feelings most of us can relate to.

WHAT'S IT TO YOU?

"A kiss is an intimate coming together of lips between two
people who want to get closer together."

T. H.

"It's that lip-smacking thing. Some are sweet, some
romantic, some obligatory (the cheek to cheek kind).
It's an international symbol for affection, caring and
warmth, sometimes better than a handshake."

S . G .

"An unbelievable magnetic force or attraction
that pulls two people together . . ."

P . D .

"It's a physical way to show little droplets
of love and affection."

K . U .

DO YOU HAVE ANY PET NAMES FOR KISSING?

Eighty percent of the women surveyed have a cute
name for a kiss. Half of them use "smooch," and some
variations of the same: smooching, smoocheroo,
smooches, smoochy-wooch, smoochie and smoochy.

Other sweet phrases and endearing words for a kiss
include:

"Show me some love"

"Let me know you love me"

"Give it to me"

"How 'bout some tongue"

"Give me some sugar"

"Gimme some love"

Kishes	Soul-kisses	Peck
Mashing	Love	Kissy
Kissy-wissy	Sugar, Sugar Smacks	Yummies

HOW DOES KISSING MAKE YOU FEEL?

"I smile whenever I think about kissing. . . .

Expectations of joy and pleasure."

L . B .

"I feel safe, comforted, warm and happy. Kissing to me

is a spontaneous gesture of fondness between

two people who truly have a bond . . . whose

relationship has meaning and significance."

J . R .

"It gives me butterflies in my stomach to think about it.
It's something you do when you have a huge crush on
someone, or else when you are madly in love."

C . L .

the history of the first "first" kiss

Despite our knowledge of ancient times, there's not much known about the genesis of kissing. The first recording of an erotic kiss was in India circa 1500 B.C. (more on this later). But the how, when and why of the first "first" kiss remains a matter of theory.

The scientific camp traces kissing to Paleolithic man. When a caveman sought a mate, he wasn't just looking for the type of girl who could clean and cook. Or had a career that made her successful in her own right. The ideal woman had to have a good immune system. And be fertile and strong.

Conditions back then were tough. And a chick from a healthy gene pool was more important than a dowry of hides and furs taken from the woolly mastodons roaming the plains. So these scruffy-looking apes would choose a lady by tasting her saliva.

Getting technical for a moment, saliva has this thinga-ma-bobby in the body called immunoglobulin (IgA). This IgA thing binds to bacteria and triggers the immune system to destroy them. Saliva also measures stress and anxiety levels, and can indicate recent traumas. Like being trampled by a herd of buffalo. Or accidentally being stabbed with a spear. You can just see the prehistoric courting ritual playing out like those reality TV dating shows!

Here are a few hypotheses from anthropologists on the first kiss:

- Cave mothers would pass already-chewed food into the mouths of their babies.
- Kissing was just a natural evolution from birth to suck our mother's breast for nourishment— simply a continual desire to breast-feed.
- Cavemen and -women would perform a "salutations" ritual of breathing closely on each other's cheeks, sharing the scent of their breath.

The more likely story? One day during this so-called breath exchange, some caveboy must have slipped, causing his lips to collide with some totally adorable cavegirl, where mouths lingered in harmony for longer than what would have been considered socially appropriate. Thus, the first real kiss as we know it.

Here's another unofficial theory to be offered on the evolution of kissing. Even those Bedrock babes understood that a kiss spoke volumes about their potential compatibility with a guy. So to get a sip of the pheremonal cocktail, they'd initiate games like "Spin the Club" or "7 Minutes in a Cave." These clever cave lassies knew a charming boy whose kisses made  them tingle would keep them happy in those damp caves at night.

Remember, ladies, the kiss has forever been the key to finding that special one. Our Stone Age sisters knew it back when.

kissing traditions that started long ago

- Ancient Rome: The Romans started all sorts of kissing traditions, like kissing at the altar to seal the "I do" deal, and kissing rings and garments of swanky officials in a sign of respect and submission. They also started the custom of husbands smooching wives when they returned home. Apparently, they were just checking to make sure their ladies hadn't been sipping wine all day!

did you know ?

In ancient days, people perfumed their mouths with myrrh to make their breath more pleasant. It was the birth of the "fresh breath" mint!

Early A.D.

- Kissing became more of a holy, reverent act used for religious rites. This is when people started kissing the Bible, an altar cloth or a baby at baptism.

Middle Ages

- The custom of using an "X" as a symbol started for those who could not read or write. Contracts would be signed with an "X," then kissed to make it binding. This is also when the submissive act of "kissing the ground you walk on" began as a way to define social standing.

♡

daily kisses XOXO

1. Next time you're kissing your sweetie, close your eyes before making lip-to-lip contact. And see if you can connect with their mouth without looking. If you miss, try again!

2. Spread a little love—kiss someone hello who might of otherwise not expected it, e.g., your dry cleaner, your doorman, your corner florist. Watch and see how they smile.

3. Keep your lips soft and moist at all times. You never know when a kiss might present itself!

2
unforgettable kisses

"For a kiss is an immortal thing. And the throb wherein
those old lips met is a living music in us yet."
GEORGE WILLIAM RUSSELL,
"AFFINITY" (1867-1935)

"Women still remember their first kiss long
after men have forgotten their last."
REMY DE GOURMONT (1858-1915)

what makes a kiss
unforgettable?

isses. If we're lucky, we'll spend a lifetime making many picture-perfect kissing memories. And like other happy moments, we'll keep a mental scrapbook, collecting these souvenirs like postcards to mark them in our hearts and minds.

But what makes a kiss unforgettable? Is it how romantic it was? How steamy and sexy? How tender or heartbreaking? How it made us "fa-shizzle" hither and yon? How it touched our hearts and souls? Or is a kiss made memorable by all sorts of pieces coming together in that ultimate collision of senses, emotions and experiences?

And have you ever wondered why is it we are able to remember momentous kisses throughout our lives—like the first boy we ever kissed, or that first one with

did you know ?

We'll spend an average of two weeks kissing in our lifetime. And the average woman will kiss seventy-nine guys before she's married. That's a lot of window-shopping!

that someone special—but can't recall what happened the other day? Maybe it's our hearts, not our heads that remember.

> " 'Kiss' rhymes to 'bliss' ", in fact as well as verse."
> LORD BYRON (1788-1824, *DON JUAN*)

UNFORGETTABLE FEELINGS

We start collecting kisses when we're young. Born wearing a "kiss me!" halo, tons of itty-bitty sweet flutters are bestowed. These droplets of love made us feel cherished, protected and adorable.

It's not until our hormones start percolating that a kiss becomes truly unforgettable. Those early, carefree kissing days can be filled with many sweet and amusing memories as we get our sea legs. Especially those "first" when our tummies felt the flutter of belly butterflies. The exhilaration of those watershed moments are remembered forever in all their glorious (or horrifying) detail.

> "Frankly, my child, I had a sudden, powerful,
> and very ignoble desire to kiss you till your lips
> were somewhat bruised."
>
> DAVID NIVEN TO MAGGIE MCNAMARA IN
> *THE MOON IS BLUE* (1953)

UNFORGETTABLE FANTASIES

Our adolescence is also when we usually start dreaming about kissing, be it with the adorable boy next store or the teen idol in our favorite magazines. Surely many of us taped a poster of some dreamy celebrity or hot rock star to the wall or ceiling above our beds believing the object of our youthful lust would ravish us with kisses among our schoolbooks and stuffed animals. The wonderful folly of the teen mind!

And those sky-high dreams might follow us into adulthood. Only now, they might feature a handsome hero man (who's a ringer for George Clooney) snatching us from the jaws of some sinister villain while simultaneously ravishing us with breathtaking kisses (and of course, our hair and makeup look glamorous despite several days in captivity!).

UNFORGETTABLE SCENTS AND TASTES

Scents or tastes, like the smell of a flower, the flavor of a chewing gum or a cologne that lingers, might also make a kiss unforgettable. I remember one hottie who made his kisses last a lifetime by "spritzing" the love notes he mailed with his aftershave. Stacking this pile of kisses on my bedside table, the supple, silky sweetness of his sexy smooches would waft over me in the dark. The fragrance of it curled my toenails!

"It was thy kiss, Love, that made me immortal."

MARGARET FULLER (1801-1880)

UNFORGETTABLE INSPIRATIONS

A kiss can be just as unforgettable for the changes it inspires in us as for the sexy, feel-good giddiness. Like the kind of kiss that would've awakened Snow White off that glass bed in that forest. A kiss like that can open a heavy, jammed door, and let the sun shine and the birds sing again. It has power, shifts our outlook, boosts our ego, and can even make us forget something like a broken heart. A kiss like that restores the faith and hope that there'll always be unforgettable kisses to be made.

most memorable kisses

When the lovely ladies from the *Kissing* survey were asked about their most memorable kisses—from their first to those special ones that have stayed locked deep inside the kissing memory banks of their hearts and souls—they had many wonderful experiences to share.

FIRST KISSES

Boy: "Wow! Where did you learn to kiss like that?"
Girl: "I used to be a tester in a bubblegum factory."
THE PENGUIN DICTIONARY OF JOKES,
EDITOR FRANK METCALF

For 50 percent of us, the first kiss happens before the age of fourteen. That's when our pituitary gland starts the crazy, hormonal happy dance. These pubescent kisses mark the precursor to sex, love and marriage (though not necessarily in that order). It forever changes our kissing: the way we think of it, the way we do it, and the way it makes us feel. Without fail, we can all bring to mind the who, when and where of that first kiss.

Here's some great "first kiss" stories played back as if they happened yesterday:

"My first smooch was when I was fifteen years old. It was quite awkward. I didn't know what I was doing . . . a lot of saliva was exchanged. Then he asked me if I could give him a hicky . . . I had no idea how to perform this deed. So I bit him. He did indeed have a mark on his throat, but it had teeth marks. So you live and learn!"

D. S.

"Seventeen years old. Four weeks into starting freshman year at college. I spotted a guy on my first day at school. He was a junior . . . and absolutely beautiful . . . One night he walked me to my dorm. We stopped and sat on a bench outside. With the chapel all lit up in front of us, on a really peaceful, clear night, he leaned in for a smooch. All I can say? Magical. Being kissed by someone you've had a crush on and wanted to kiss, particularly when you thought it would never happen, is pretty powerful stuff. He and I were a couple for three and half years after that."

C. C.

"My first kiss was seven minutes in heaven with LL in sixth grade. Didn't know to breath through my nose and

did you know ?

Puberty actually starts with a kiss. Scientists have discovered the torrent of hormones triggering sexual maturity are set off by a gene called Kiss-1. This gene, which produces a protein called kisspeptin, switches on the part of the brain that then sends the signal to another important gene called GPR54. That gene makes all the hormones needed to physically mature. Yahoo! Let the kissing begin!

when he came in for the kiss, I held my breath . . . after
thirty seconds or so, I started squeaking."

G . L .

Even our sexy, female, celebrity sisters remember their
first kiss. And they're just as exciting, uncertain, awkward and colorfully detailed as our own:

"My first real kiss was at a girlfriend's sweet sixteen party.
I kissed the most gorgeous boy in high school, the guy
everyone fancied, and I was so overcome, I cried . . ."

LISA KUDROW

"I was twelve. His name was Nicky and he had braces. We
were in the backyard, and I'm like, You wanna do it, you
wanna do it? Well, okay, let's do it. And then we did. It was
just awful. But then it was darkness, saliva and tongue."

CHARLIZE THERON

"The first boy I ever kissed was Ronny Howard in
the fifth grade. He had real white, blond hair and
sky-blue eyes. I wrote his name all over my sneakers

and on the playground, I used to take off the top
part of my school uniform and chase him around."

MADONNA

REPLAYING THAT MOST SPECIAL KISS

When asked about that most special kiss, most women refer to the first with a past love or the love they're with. Others might think of unexpected moments. Or even the ones that weren't meant to be. Whatever the occasion or circumstance, they're kisses that can be taken down from a shelf and relived at any moment.

"The first kiss after we were pronounced
husband and wife."

B. F.

"My first kiss with my husband . . . Actually, it was the
third time that we were together and our first night
together . . . We kissed each other everywhere on our
bodies for about five hours nonstop while we were
listening to jazz music. It was when we realized that we

had incredible chemistry for one another . . . It was a
whirlwind. And it remains a memory that we both share."

T . W .

"It's always the first one with the guy you really like.
It's fresh, new, soaring . . ."

E . G .

"Probably the first kiss with my now boyfriend shared
on his rooftop . . . I remember my insides started
to rise and I was all aflutter!"

J . R .

"A scuba instructor while on vacation in the Caribbean.
Wet and steamy!"

G . J .

"I think I'm supposed to be the good wife and say my
husband. But let's not be the good wife just for today,
and I'll say it was the kiss from the most handsome
Italian man I had ever seen! . . ."

M . L .

"Kissing this redhead on the street and literally feeling
butterflies in my stomach. Then a car drove by and
gave us the thumbs-up!"

F . S .

SOME EMBARRASSING KISSES

Not all kisses are idyllic "I'm running slow-mo in a field
with my hair blowing in the wind looking like a cover
girl" kind of kisses. Some are downright clumsy. Goofy.
Even painful! Others are embarrassing not so much for
the kiss itself, but the who, where and when (like a co-
worker in the copier room at an office party!). We've all
been there in some way shape or form.

"My honey and I were lying in bed, and as he came to kiss
me on the back of the neck, I spun my head around and
bopped him in the face pretty hard. His nose practically
started bleeding. I felt so bad, but made up for it later."

K . L .

"I was on a blind date with this really cute guy. He took
me to dinner and the movies. I had a feeling he was going

to kiss me. We kept kind of looking at each other then
turning our heads away to watch the movie. And then
he made the move, but just as he came into kiss me, I let
out the tiniest soda burp. I was so embarrassed!!!"

M. N.

"My boyfriend and I were hanging around listening
to CD's, and he started kissing me before I could
take the gum I was chewing out of my mouth, so I
hid it in the back. The kissing got pretty intense,
and somehow the gum slipped into my
throat. I practically choked!"

G. F.

famous screen kisses—big and small

"I'd love to kiss you
but I just washed my hair."
BETTE DAVIS (*CABIN IN THE COTTON*, 1932)

DREAMY MOVIE KISSES

There have been numerous polls listing the best movie kisses of all times. Without fail, the gold standard atop  of every list for eternity (always has been and will always be) is *Gone With the Wind*. When Rhett grabs Scarlett off the carriage as Atlanta burns against the fiery orange sky and declares, "Scarlett, I love you more than I've ever loved any woman. And I've waited longer for you than I've ever waited for any woman. Here's a soldier of the South that loves

did you know

In a Gallup poll, 25 percent of respondents picked *Gone With the Wind* as the movie with the most memorable screen smooches. "I do declare, that Rhett Butler and Scarlett O'Hara are as hot as ever!"

you. You're the woman who's sending a soldier to his death with a beautiful memory. Scarlett, kiss me, kiss me once," we die in his arms.

> "I want you to faint. That's what you were meant for.
> None of those fools you've ever known have
> kissed you like this, have they?"
> RHETT TO SCARLETT
> (*GONE WITH THE WIND*, 1939)

To get a list of the most memorable movie kisses, these are the ones that famous movie critic Joel Siegel from *Good Morning America* ranked best:

1. *Gone With the Wind*
2. *From Here to Eternity*
3. *The Princess Bride*
4. *Jerry Maguire*
5. *Top Gun*
6. *Lost in Translation*
7. *Intolerable Cruelty*
8. *Spider-Man*
9. *Life Is Beautiful*
10. *Titanic*

11. *To Catch a Thief*
12. *Body Heat*
13. *Witness*
14. *Casablanca*

We all have our favorite screen kisses—moments that inspire, make us weep for joy and happiness, or cry out with longing and sorrow. These kisses touch our emotions no matter how many times we watch them.

Along with *Gone With the Wind*, *Casablanca* and *Jerry Maguire*, the girls in the survey listed a range of movies, some sweet and innocent, others hot and steamy.

Fuzzy & Fun	A Wee Heartbreaking	Sexxxy Sexxxy
Dirty Dancing	The Notebook	Ghost
Beauty &	The English Patient	The Big Easy
The Beast	Dr. Zhivago	Unfaithful
Sixteen Candles	An Affair	The Piano
The Sound	to Remember	9 1/2 Weeks
of Music		
Pillow Talk		
Bridget Jones'		
Diary		

There are some real standouts here. Like the *The Sound of Music*. That first kiss between Captain Von Trapp and the erstwhile nun Maria from the abbey is one of the sweetest, most tender screen smooches. When they hold hands and sing their first words of love to each other in the gazebo—"*Somewhere in my youth and childhood, I must have done something good,*" their silhouette forms a heart against the blue, dewy, moonlit night. It's magic . . . pure magic.

did you know ?

Watching movies boost our hormone levels. Depending on the content, a movie can get you feeling frisky (or in the mood to fight). Sentimental movies like *Bridges of Madison County* can make your progesterone go up more than 10 percent. And since progesterone helps reduce stress and anxiety, you'll be feeling more mellow and randy. We should watch romantic movies every day!

SURPRISING AND NOT SO SURPRISING TV KISSES

TV has had some very unforgettable kisses, too. Between series, movies, live award shows and events, we've seen a variety of high (and low) kissing moments.

There've been hilarious, unbelievable, long-awaited and groundbreaking kisses, ones that shock, rock and make you go "yikes"!

Every once in a while a TV kiss comes along that breaks new ground. The 2005 made-for-TV movie *Their Eyes Were Watching God* had one super-racy, sexy, sugar

did you know ?

One of the longest kisses ever recorded happened on *The Ricki Lake Show* on January 28th, 2002. Louisa Almodovar and Rich Langly of New Jersey kissed for a record thirty hours, fifty-nine minutes and twenty-seven seconds! Did they take a breather during "Now, a Message from Our Sponsor"?

DO YOU REMEMBER THESE MEMORABLE TV MOMENTS?

Year	Show	Kissers	Rating
1968	*Star Trek*	Capt. Kirk & Lt. Uhura	xxx
1972	*All in the Family*	Sammy Davis Jr. & Archie	xxxx
1973	*The Brady Bunch*	Marcia & Davy Jones	xxx
1983	*Cheers*	Sam & Diane	xxxx
1994	*Friends*	Joey & Chandler	xx
1995	*Friends*	Ross & Rachel	xxxxx
1997	*Ellen*	Ellen & Laura	xxxx
2000	*Will & Grace*	Jack & Will	xxxx
2000	Democratic Convention	Al & Tipper Gore	1/2 an x
2003	Oscars	Halle & Adrian	xxxx & 1/2
2003	*Dawson's Creek*	Jack & Doug	xxx & 1/2
2003	Video Music Awards	Madonna & Britney	x & 1/2
2005	*All My Children*	Bianca & Maggie	xxxx
2005	*The O.C.*	Marissa & Alex	xxx

Rating Scale

x	Poor	Get thee to a kissing guru!
xx	Needs Work	Buy *Kissing* for some tips!
xxx	Not Bad	Okay, but keep practicing!
xxxx	Really Good	Ooo, la la, you could turn a few heads!
xxxxx	Super Hot	Call 911! That house is on fire!!!

did you know ?

In classic '50s and '60s TV, network censors required a couple who kissed on a bed or couch to keep one foot on the floor. Even Lucy and Ricky—and they were married in real life!

smack between the characters (played by Halle Berry and Michael Ealy). In a scene that might have been censored not too long ago, they sensually lick each other's lips and tongues. There's even some very "come hither" dancing, and slurping of a lychee nut out of Halle's hand. My, oh, my!

who would you give your eyeteeth to kiss?

"All really nice girls wonder why men don't try to kiss
them. They know they shouldn't want them to and they
know they must act insulted if they do, but just the same,
they wish the men would try."

MARGARET MITCHELL

(*GONE WITH THE WIND*, 1939)

We all have fantasies of being ravished by some hunky
hottie, real or make-believe. When the women who
took the *Kissing* survey were asked who they'd want to
be stranded with on a desert island (which, of course,
has a day spa to keep them looking fresh and lovely at
all times), they revealed they'd be happy to roll in the
warm tropical waters with:

The Classics	The Neo-Classics
Cary Grant	George Clooney
Clint Eastwood	Dennis Quaid
Sean Connery	Pierce Brosnan
Paul Newman	Harrison Ford
Robert Redford	Tom Cruise
Clark Gable	Russell Crowe

The BMOC	The Young Turks
Brad Pitt	Ryan Gosling
Jude Law	Sean Bean
Benicio Del Toro	Olivier Martinez
Denzel Washington	Orlando Bloom
Colin Firth	Colin Farrell

Those men all have serious *kiss-a-risma*. Yum-meeee with a capital Y. M. E.!

Even celebs have their own memorable kissing highlights:

"It was certainly when I kissed Bob DeNiro in *Casino*."
SHARON STONE (*PEOPLE*, 11/29/04)

"In *Pretty in Pink*, I kiss Andrew McCarthy after he asks
me to go to the prom. Some people think it's
The Breakfast Club one with Judd Nelson at the end.
But I think that *Pretty in Pink* was the sexiest."

MOLLY RINGWALD

"He's a very good kisser. . . . Those kinds of scenes
you can't help but feel vulnerable."

MARY MCDONNELL ON KISSING

KEVIN COSTNER

"Orson Welles kissed me with his soul, never with his lips."

EARTHA KITT

memorable
screen kisses

- 1896: The first screen kiss ever is shown
  in a movie appropriately called *The Kiss*.
- 1929: In the film *Don Juan,* starring
  John Barrymore, the eponymous hero

averages a kiss every fifty-three seconds, for 191 kisses in total.

- 1941: The longest lip-lock in film history takes

daily kisses xoxo

1. Rent a couple of your favorite romantic movies. Watch the kissing scenes closely. And take note of the style and technique. When you've got it down, plan a candlelit night with your sweetie, and reenact those steamy, tender kisses, move for move! Your "pookie bear" will be glad you're such a movie buff!

2. Give a "thank you" kiss to the folks at your neighborhood video store for bringing great kissing entertainment to the privacy of your home! Oh, and grab some popcorn while you're there. And maybe a box of chocolate-covered caramels, too!

3. You're never too old for a little silliness. Next time you see the sexy face of your most favorite kiss-a-liscious celebrity in a magazine or on TV, blow 'em a kiss! Your sweet sugar will zip magically from your lips to theirs (like email through an Internet cable). They will receive it. Honest.

place between Jane Wyman and Regis Toomey in the 1941 film *You're In the Army Now*. That kiss went on for three minutes and five seconds. That's some puckerin' up!

* 1968: American TV features its first interracial kiss between Captain James T. Kirk and Lieutenant Uhuru on *Star Trek*. As scripted, Spock was to lock lips with Uhuru. But when that Captain Kirk, turned *T. J. Hooker*, turned *Rescue 911*, turned *Boston Legal*'s Denny Crane heard, he said something along the lines of, "No way! If there's gonna be any kissing of Uhuru, it will be by the Captain!"

♡

3
what makes a great kiss?

"'Where should one use perfume?' a young woman asked.

'Wherever one wants to be kissed,' I said."

COCO CHANEL (1883-1971)

When asked what goes into making a great, memorable kiss, the ladies from the *Kissing* survey said that a beautiful kiss that lingers should bring together a combination of who, what and where ingredients.

Who: Your Partner Should . . .

- Taste good
- Have a light touch, e.g., avoids shoving his tongue down your throat
- Hold back just a bit before the contact, then light touch
- Let you kiss back
- Have enough talent to make you hungry for more
- Give you their complete and undivided attention

What: The Kiss Should Be Made up Of . . .

- Soft, gentle, juicy, warm, slightly parted lips
- Some tongue
- Chemistry—the chemical connection/reaction it creates between the two of you
- Synchronicity—timing is everything!
- The perfect combination of tenderness and toughness
- Electricity and spontaneity
- Safety and real intimacy

- Total newness
- Genuine feeling

Other responses about what makes kisses good enough for the memory bank:

> "Both lips . . . relaxed with time . . . passion . . .
> caring . . . I love a "stolen" kiss—
> an unexpected kiss as you pass your mate . . .
> a kiss on the neck that makes you
> tingle from the location of the kiss
> down to your toes . . ."
>
> Q. B.

> "Lips that appreciate your lips. A softness and
> pressure on the lips that mounts and
> changes along with development of feeling.
> A stroking and caressing of lips on lips with
> a few gentle nibbles thrown in, and of course
> the intimate tongue that tastes and
> explores and wants more."
>
> G. S.

"When two people are kissing for the same reason, and feeling the same emotions at the exact moment."

L . K .

"When you feel like you're speaking through your kisses."

B . N .

WHERE GREAT KISSING HAPPENS

on our bodies

Great kisses are not just about kisses to the lips, but the ones we love to feel on our bodies. Most women like kisses "anywhere and everywhere." A few favorite spots are the neck and ears. The corners of their mouth and stomach are lovely, too. For goose bumps, it's the back of the neck under their hair. That spot can really kick you into a frenzy!

Some ladies like being kissed on the small of their back and curve of their waist. Others find the underside of the forearm or inside of the ankle to be super sensitive to a kiss. Yes, kissing is good pretty much anywhere.

And kisses to different parts of your body can mean different things:

If You're Kissed . . .	It Means . . .
On the hand	Friendship
On the nose	You're cute
On the cheek	I need you
On the neck	I love you
With eyes closed	I'm in love with you
With eyes open	I'm watching where your hands are going

in what location

"When I first see my lover outside my apartment where he picks me up. Then when he drops me off, we walk to the river and kiss while watching the water rush madly by us."

R . E .

When we think of exciting, romantic, comfortable places to kiss, the survey girls say they'll pucker up anywhere. On the couch. In bed. On the car. At the front door. On a chair lift. In the shower. In front of a breathtaking view. And on and on.

But the actual place is not as important as the spontaneity—*"kissing should be done on the fly."* It's all about wherever and whenever the mood strikes. And seizing that moment with passion.

Some other tantalizing, romantic locales to kiss might be:

- On the beach—under a full moon or around a bonfire
- While cooking in the kitchen—breakfast, lunch or dinner
- At an airport—preferably kissing hello, not good-bye!
- In an elevator—just make sure there are no security cameras!
- On a boat—the waves can rock you!
- At a great site, e.g., Niagra Falls, the Grand Canyon

- In a park—on a bench or in a horse-drawn carriage
- A romantic city, e.g., Paris, Venice

Bottom line, it doesn't matter where you're doing it, just as long as you're doing it!

♡

4
kissing 101:
the fundamentals
of great kissing

"You must not kiss and tell."

WILLIAM COSGROVE (*LOVE FOR LOVE*)

Kissing. It's an activity we spend much time practicing and perfecting. Some succeed to dizzying heights of skill and talent. Others are happily enthusiastic participants. No matter how adept, many kissers seek to improve their talent and finesse to seductively impress.

But how do we become good kissers? Oddly enough, this is one of the more significant rites of passage we're generally not taught by our role models. They teach us other important things. Like reading. (I still recall the moment of making the connection between sounding out the letters to form a word.) Riding a bike. Swimming. Driving. Sewing. Even how babies are made. But not kissing.

early kissing instructions

Most of us invariably learn to kiss passively through observation. Thank God for TV and the movies. If we're lucky, we might have an older sibling give us the scoop. But for the most part, without any official how-to instructions, we're thrown into the deep end of the pool with no water wings, and expected to swim.

"'Watch this.' Nancy grabbed the pillow and embraced it. When she was done, she threw the pillow back on the

bed. 'It's important to experiment, so when the
time comes you're all ready. I'm going to be a
great kisser some day.' "
FROM *ARE YOU THERE GOD? IT'S ME,
MARGARET* BY JUDY BLUME (1970)

All I knew was to close my eyes, lean in and touch the
boy on his mouth with mine. Forget about what to do
with the tongue. And the saliva factor—whoa, how do
you keep that under control? It would be some time before getting this down pat.

did you know ?

In an American opinion poll, 41 percent of people keep their
eyes closed when they kiss. 20 percent admit to peeking. And
8 percent keep their eyes open. Of the girls surveyed, 71 percent
said they kiss with eyes mostly closed but also open. It's nice to
look into your honey's eyes from time to time!

"Whoever named it necking was a
poor judge of anatomy."
GROUCHO MARX (1895-1977)

mastering a talent

Then like the magic of connecting letters to make a word, I remember realizing when my kisses seemed to have some special effect. While kissing this guy, he started blurting out things like he was "being swept away by an ocean wave," and "drowning in a sea of kisses." His sound effects and poetry filled me with a great sense of satisfaction.

"Her lips suck forth my soul."
CHRISTOPHER MARLOWE (1564-1593)

Today, if someone asks, "Are you a good kisser?", I offer with a wink and a smile that my Armenian and Greek heritage fosters an innate talent (people from the "kebab belt" are naturally good kissers).

survey says...

When asked how they rated themselves as kissers:

a. Red hot (if they did say so themselves)

b. Pretty good but open to suggestions

c. Short on technique yet enthusiastic

d. Other

Happily, 60 percent of the gals feel pretty confident about their kissing. Forty percent rate themselves as "red hot," even "unforgettable" kissers. Major "props" for their certainty!

just when you think you know it all . . .

So it would come as a surprise one day that some guy would have the nerve to critique my kissing. He seemed rather delighted at first, commenting, "Madame, that's some impressive kissing." But the next time we locked lips, he made other remarks. They were less than complimentary: "You kiss like a guppy. Don't open your mouth so wide. Don't use so much tongue." Guess there really is a first time for everything!

Appreciating there's not a lot of official kissing instruction in our lives, and that we're never too good to learn a thing or two, here are some tips and exercises to help you brush up on your kissing. Remember, you're never too old to improve your pucker.

kissing makeover tips and techniques

"I'm fond of kissing. It's part of my job.
God sent me down to kiss a lot of people."
CARRIE FISHER

Here are three steps for fabulous kissing that will take you from decent kisser to dazzling 5-karat kisser that will make them "ooh" and aah"!

STEP #1: GETTING YOUR PUCKER INTO SHAPE

"A soft lip would tempt you to an eternity of kissing."

BEN JOHNSON (1573-1637)

The first step to perfecting the art of great kissing is to make sure your luscious lips, mouth and tongue are in fine form, because one of the keys to being utterly *smoochable* is keeping those elements primed. Just as we work out our abs and butts, our tongues need exercise for better grace and flexibility.

Here are some ways to get that tongue of yours ready. Have fun with these solo or with a friend. Some are a little tough. But they'll all get you into super shape for slinky kisses.

on your own exercises

- *The Wrap*: Put a piece of wrapped candy in your mouth, e.g., a caramel or mint. Try unwrapping the candy with your tongue. No hands!
- *The Stretch*: Stretch your tongue out as far as it will go. Try touching the tip of your nose (or as

far as possible). Do the same with your tongue to your chin. Repeat a bunch of times (this is good to do during a commercial or while you're standing in front of the microwave heating up a snack).

- *The Flex*: Try to make your tongue as tall as possible. Then as flat as possible. Then as tall as possible again. Do this while your first coat of nail polish is drying. Then do it again when the second coat is drying.

buddy exercises

Recommended with someone you're already pretty sexy with:

- *The Hoola-Hoop*: Use your tongue to circle your partner's lips. Go 'round and 'round a couple of times. Switch directions. Then take turns. Beware, this can get you heated up lickety-split!
- *Rock Star Kiss*: Stand about three inches apart.

Extend your tongues until they touch. Think of the famous rock 'n' roll band KISS. Don't be surprised if you start playing "air" guitar!

- *Tongue Suckers*: Stick out your tongue while your partner sucks on your tongue to stretch it as far as possible. Take turns. And no biting!

Your tongue might feel a little sore after all this stimulation. Like any muscle, just give it a rest, and you'll be good to go again soon.

STEP #2: MASTER THE KISSING COMMANDMENTS

So let's review the fundamental things you need to do to spruce up your kissing and ensure they're of the highest quality:

1. *Get Mellow Yellow* A good kiss comes from the mood within. Yes, you have to know what to do with your lips and tongue. But your mind and spirit need to be relaxed. In the words of that

sizzling girl group En Vogue, "Free your mind, and the rest will follow." Empty your head from the static of the day. Take a deep breath. Exhale. Just think about kissing. And being kissed. A wee stressed? Or not feeling super-duper? Don't pass on kissing. The magic elixir of a kiss does wonders for whatever ails you. Like waving a wand. Poof!

2. *Floss and Gloss*—The mouth and lips are sacred things. Treat them with utmost care, because soft *kiss-a-luscious* lips and a fresh mouth will render you most *smoochable*. They won't be able to get enough of your kisses!

    * On the mouth—Since you never want your kisses dinged for an avoidable foul, floss, gargle and brush daily like you're the poster girl for the American Dental Association. Drink plenty of water, too. If you're a smoker, a little gum or a mint is helpful. Just don't have any of this in your mouth when kissing (unless you plan to share it with that person, which can be fun!)

    * On the lips—This is the first thing a guy is going to feel when you come in for the kiss. So to make a supple, sensual impression, moisturize

your lips with an emollient several times a day, especially before bedtime.

** What's also a must is some shiny lip gloss. All girls should wear a little for that extra shimmer to keep their lips looking as juicy and ripe as a piece of fresh mango, even it they're just running out in their sweats to do some errands. Always put your best lips forward!

** And just before you kiss, run your tongue over your lips to slightly moisten. If you know you'll be kissing, go easy on the lipstick. It can get a little messy. You don't want your partner wearing it.

3. *Create A Cozy Nook*—Kissing is pretty much good anytime, anywhere, but for yummy canoodling, curl up on a fluffy couch, comfy bed or cushy window seat. Light a few candles. Play nice soft, sexy music (Sade is good). And snuggle up in their lap and arms. Chat a little about the day. Sip a little wine. Nibble on some cheese (snack and beverages optional). Enjoy reconnecting and the anticipation of the kissing to come.

4. *Get Lip to Lip*—When you start, less is more. Make soft, light contact with your lips. Kiss their lips

gently. Stroke their lips with yours. Alternate kissing the corner of their mouth, nose and cheeks. Then come back to their lips. Rest on the lips a little longer this time. Part your lips. Maybe suck on their lip. Or caress it with your tongue. Do this while stroking the back of their neck. Or running your fingers through their hair. Or touching their cheek. Even kissing their neck in that little crook where the collarbone meets.

5. *Turn up the Heat*—As you start feeling the *fuego* (that's hot for "fire"), get more succulent and luscious. Introduce more tongue. Brush the inside of their mouth with your tongue. Maybe suck on their tongue. Suck their upper and lower lips, too. Take a breather. Kiss them deeply but without tongue. Mix it up a little. Look intently into their eyes. Continue stroking and caressing in nice places. Feel the chemistry bubbling as your scents mingle to create your exclusive fragrance. Whisper how you want to give them more pleasure in places hither and yon. Enjoy the passion you inspire in one another.

And while you're doing all this wonderful smooching, be mindful of a few things to avoid killing the kiss:

6. *Watch the Tongue*: No one likes kissing a flickering, tongued serpent. Don't slide your tongue down their throat like the electric snake used to clear the clog in a sink. You could actually gag someone.

7. *Relax the Tongue*: It's not just the slithering tongue that's a turn-off. It's the stiff one. The tongue is a muscle. Keep it loose. Just give a little. Then a little more. Don't slam into someone's mouth. You're a nice girl kissing a guy, not a S.W.A.T. commander raiding a safe house. "Easy does it" works all the time.

8. *Hold Steady*: Avoid weaving your head from side to side, or bobbing back and forth. You could end up accidentally banging a nose or knock out a few teeth. Ouch. Remember, kissing shouldn't be painful, nor require first aid.

9. *Don't Stiffen*: Kissing a statue or wooden board isn't pleasant either. While you don't want to bobble and wobble, a little poise and charm is required.

french-kissing tips

French kissing is like eating ice cream—not the kind from those two nice boys Ben and Jerry, but that creamy custard that comes gently swirling out of a machine. Caress your partner's tongue with your tongue the way you'd enjoy your ice cream. Lick it slowly. Stroke it. Suck it. Flick the tip of their tongue with yours. Roll your tongue along their lips. Or playfully twirl your tongue through theirs. Take pleasure in it. Your mouths will both be filled with immense silky satisfaction.

Be soft and gentle. Move slowly from his mouth to his ears and neck, then back to his mouth again. Tilt your head back gracefully when he kisses your neck. Smiling and laughing in between kisses is nice, too. A little humor always makes for good kissing. So be loose (how "loose" is up to you!).

10. *Manage the Mouth and Saliva*: The mouth has an amazing ability to open and close. It can expand as big as your fist, or be sealed shut. So be mindful

of how wide or narrow you go. No one likes to have their face engulfed by an echoing cavern. Airtight lip-locks aren't pleasant either. Use your judgment depending on the size of their mouth.

As for the wetness factor, we don't come equipped with that little, slurping saliva-sucking hoosa-ma-ghiggy the dentist uses. Make sure you swallow from time to time. There's nothing more embarrassing than spraying someone with your spittle.

Most of all, remember to have fun. Kissing is more about the energy and spirit than the technique. Your confidence and ease will create kisses that are happily received. Your magic princess power will make them immortal.

STEP #3: MODELING YOUR NEW KISSING "WARDROBE"

Between the working out and 101 refresher, let's look at several kisses you should perfect.

Just as a girl needs certain things in her closet, e.g., a

black cocktail dress, "to die for" pumps, and an undergarment of the lacy kind (even if you prefer cotton for the everyday, you should always have a frilly bra and panty set for that hint of sassiness), she needs a repertoire of kisses.

To ensure you are a girl that's definitely the kissing kind, master these essential moves:

1. *The Happy Hello*: This is the "greet when you meet" kiss. Whether it happens on a street corner, a restaurant, party or your doorstep, it should be enthusiastic and warm.

    *   Start with a smile and happy hello: "Hi, so happy to see you." Or "Hi, so happy you're home."

    *   Put your arms around his neck. Pull him toward you for a little hug. Stroke his hair. Or rub the back of his neck. These should be brief flutters of touch.

    *   Give a soft, supple kiss to the lips. This should linger for a second or two. Your mouth can be loosely closed or slightly open. This lets him know there'll be more kissing to come! No

matter how busy your day has been, or how occupied you might be at the moment, take the time for a *Happy Hello* to reconnect.

The *Happy Hello* is also an ideal way to warm the air after a little tiff. Remember, guys can be feeling a wee uncertain, too. So put them at ease. The bump in the road will be behind you in a jiffy.

> "I say, when there are spats, kiss and make up before
> the day is done and live to fight another day."
>
> REVEREND RANDOLPH RAY
>
> (*NEW YORK WORLD TELEGRAM*, 1956)

2. *The Sultry So-Long*: If the *Happy Hello* is a delicately suggestive greeting, the *Sultry So-Long* headlines what he's in for when he returns. Be it off to work, a trip or quick errand, he'll be back in no time!

   - Move in close. Wrap your arms around his back, and press your body against his. Maybe say something corny but cheeky like, "Hey, here's one for the road," or, "This should keep a smile on your face all day."

- Bring your mouth to his. Press your lips against his with a medium amount of pressure. Your mouth should be slightly open.
- Run your tongue ever so lightly along his top lip. Or gently suck his bottom lip.
- Pull away. Then kiss him on the cheek. Not the way you kiss your grandfather, but the kind that reminds him where he gets good lovin'.

3. *The Dirty Dancer*: This is the kind of kissin' that can lead to other sexy things. You're at a bar, club or party, or maybe enjoying a romantic night at home with Barry White and Marvin Gaye. You're feeling frisky and know what the night will likely bring. So get a little randy!

- Stand close in front of your honey. Put your arms around his waist. Maybe suggestively pinch or squeeze his butt. Or push your hand into his back pocket. Even slip your fingers inside the top of his beltline. If you're dancing, this is a perfect way to hold on and sway back and forth in your groove.

- When the air feels ripe, come in for a kiss. Start on the side of his mouth. Then bring your lips to his. Gently suck, even nibble, his lower lip. Caress the inside of his mouth with your tongue. It should be a brief, soft sweep. Keep your hands around his waist or resting on his hips.

- Before going in for the deep kiss, bump and grind a little at the hips. Throw back your head. Even arch your back (be careful, you don't want to end up in the chiropractor's office!). When you're face to face, come in really close. But don't kiss just yet. Look him in the eye and let your partner enjoy your suggestive moves. Feel the pizzazz between you, and anticipate what's coming. Then get into some deep kissing. If you're not into public displays, save this move for the bedroom.

"To avoid eye contact, kiss."

MASON COOLEY

(*CITY APHORISMS*, NEW YORK, 1989)

4. *The Purring Pussy Cat*: Every girl has many wonderful facets to her personality. We can shift seamlessly from sexy diva to itty-bitty kitty. So this is the perfect kind of smoochin' to do when lying in bed or snuggled up on the couch.

- Wrap yourself around him. Look him in the eyes. Caress his face, and kiss his lips, cheeks, neck and forehead gently.

- Don't use any tongue. Keep all the sensuality in your lips—the way you slowly draw your lips across his face, the way you softly press against his mouth, the way you nuzzle his neck and ears. Let the shared air hang between you.

- Pause for a moment in between these sweet, intimate kisses. Whisper in his ear. Tell him how you want to give him pleasure. And when he kisses you back, sigh a little. You should feel like a pussycat purring contentedly in the warmth of the golden sun.

mood makers
& breakers

"If your lips itch, you shall kiss somebody."

JOHN MILTON (1608-1674)

Of the many things covered in the *Kissing* survey, one important topic was moods—making them and breaking them.

MAKING IT

When asked, "What gets you in the mood to kiss?", many of the girls said tequila! Do a few shots, or drink a couple of frozen strawberry margaritas, and you'll be shakin' your groove thing all over!

While most said they're in the mood to kiss pretty much all of the time, the ladies are wooed to kiss by a combination of emotions and certain ambiance that really gets their "mojo in hojo":

- Feeling love—the most cozy sensation sure to inspire romantic "you're the only one for me" kissing
- Being complimented, e.g., "You're so sexy, I can't believe guys don't throw themselves at you when you are walking down the street."
- Being made to laugh—a good joke or sense of humor makes for fun kissing
- Trust—essential to intimate kissing
- Terms of endearment—it's nice to have a pet name that you share with a certain someone
- Close physical contact—when the electricity is palpable, it's a real turn-on
- Good conversation—nothing more stimulating than watching a sexy mouth doing yadda yadda yadda, and thinking about kissing it
- Time apart—absence does make the heart grow fonder (and the kissing hotter!)
- Just seeing their sweetie—watching them walk down the street or into a party can get you purring

survey says...

When asked what they did when they were in the mood to kiss:

a. Make the first move

b. Let someone else make the first move

c. Play it by ear

d. Grab a pillow cuz there ain't no one worth kissing!

Forty-eight percent of girls would make the first move—*"Life is too short. If the signals are there, go for it!"* Thirty-seven percent would play it by ear. And 15 percent would let someone else make the first move.

Of course, romantic standards like wine, soft music, scented candles and a beautiful moon go far in creating that certain "let's kiss" vibe. Dinner out, good food and a chick flick help, too!

BREAKING IT

So what can put the kibosh on a perfectly wonderful moment?

- A stupid remark from your love bug, e.g., a mention you've put on weight
- An argument or anger
- Interruptions, e.g., phone or doorbell ringing, child crying, dog barking
- A crotchety mood—Oscar the Grouch should stay home
- Bad breath, e.g., onions, nicotine, stale beer and alcohol
- Stinky hygiene—when did you last shower and wash your hair? *Foochie-rama!*
- Razor stubble—ouch, beard burn can leave a face, chin and nose looking sunburned!
- A yucky location—if my feet are sticking to the floor, how can your kisses make me float on air?
- Sloppiness—sloppy saliva, sloppy drunkenness, sloppy tongue . . . just plain sloppiness

- No finesse, e.g., dry and quick, tight-lipped, head straight, no flow
- Too much enthusiasm—we don't need to be kissing the male cheerleading squad!
- Too much tongue or no tongue—everything in moderation, even tongue
- No spirit or love—gotta have a little love . . .
- No chemistry or creativity—that kiss might be dead in the water before you even start!

Kissing the wrong man or looking for more than just a kiss can kill the moment, too. Getting caught in the action could also be a downer. But then again, that could also be what makes it memorable!

foods that turn you on—creating the mood with some tasty treats

If you want to ensure a night (or day) filled with scrumptious kissing, try serving some kissing-friendly snacks. That thing about "aphrodisiacs" getting your love vibe bopping is true. Some foods have specific scents that enhance a romantic mood. Other foods have ingredients that cause your brain to shoot all those sexy signals to tropical parts below your equator line.

> "I love thee like pudding; if thou wert pie I'd eat thee."
>
> JOHN RAY (1628-1705)

There are, of course, the classic love snacks—oysters and chocolate. Oysters have zinc, which pumps the blood.

survey says...

If your honey is in the mood to kiss but you're not, do you:

a. Push him away

b. Give him a little peck

c. Act like a good sport and try to get into it

d. You're never not in the mood to kiss

Thirty-two percent declared they were never not in the mood for a kiss—*"Life is too damn short!"* Forty percent would be a good sport about it—*"A great kiss doesn't always have to take a long time. Take a break and get into it unless the house is burning down!"* That's a philosophy to kiss by! Twenty percent would respond with a little peck. And 8 percent would expect him to work a little harder to get you in the mood.

And chocolate has that uplifting chemical phenylethylamine (PEA for short), which mimics being totally googoo-eyed. Hence, chocolate on Valentine's Day. Between the compounds and the taste, chocolate makes for very sensuous kissing. And if a little chocolate melts on your mouth (and not in your hands), just think how nice it would be to have someone nibble it off!

So what to serve? If you go for "tried 'n true," try:

- Oysters
- Champagne and caviar
- Chocolate—eat it straight or melt it down for dipping some fruit (strawberries work well) or cookies
- Fruit, e.g., seedless oranges and grapes, fresh figs, strawberries or any fresh berries in whipped cream
- Ice cream—you can practice your French kissing technique while eating ice cream

For more unexpected treats that will get your blood pumping and feeling *smooch-a-liscious*, try this:

- For guys: pumpkin pie paired with lavender, black licorice, donuts, cheese pizza and buttered popcorn
- For girls: licorice candy, cucumbers or banana nut bread

did you know ❓

Those oh-so-tasty chocolate Hershey's® Kisses got their name from the machine that makes them. When the chocolate drops out, it looks like it's kissing the conveyor belt. It even makes a puckering sound! No wonder they are such a sweet treat!

You might even want to try herbs like ginseng, gingko biloba and yohimbine. These also increase blood flow and affect the brain's chemistry. Food prepared with spices like cayenne pepper can get the love juices boiling, too.

As for Spanish Fly, this legendary love drug is a wee dangerous. Its real name is cantharides, and it's extracted from dried beetle dung (*foochie!*). It can do things like cause urinary infections. Or burn the inside of your mouth and throat. Not very pleasant. So proceed with caution here!

If you're feeling really exotic and adventurous, try deer antlers, sandalwood, Alder bark, Gypsyweed rose petals and patchouli (fragrant oils from a mint shrub tree found in India). But unless you live in the forest, or an open game reserve, these might be hard to come by.

Great kissing is also what you make it. So anything you serve can be the menu for sexy kissing. It's all in the attitude!

> "Kissing a pretty girl is like opening a bottle of olives.
> After the first one, the rest come easy."
> ANONYMOUS

legendary kissing

- Sixth century: In India, Buddhists and Hindus began the practice of Tantrism. This was believed to transform the human body into a mystical one where human union became a sacred act. They must have been doing some magical kissing!

- Early eleventh century: In Japan, one of the earliest and greatest romance novels is written—*The Tale of the Genji*—by Lady Murasaki Shikibu. She describes the refined but libidinous kissing court life in Japan.

- 1142: *The Ananga-Raga* is written in India. Similar to the *Kama Sutra*, this love manual details the latest "how-to" techniques for erotic mouth-to-mouth kissing. It was intended to keep the love flame hot so couples would remain faithful forever. Even ancient society had its temptations!

- 17th century: Martin von Kempe creates one of the first known encyclopedia of kisses, in Germany. It's packed with up to 1,040 references of excerpts from classical, biblical, medical, legal and other sources. What a scholar!

♡

daily kisses XOXO

1. Transport yourself and your sweetie to the "Kissing Kasbah" far, far away. Drape your living room or bedroom with silk scarves. Toss a couple of pillows on the floor. Light a few sandalwood candles. Dress like a genie in a bottle. Serve up fresh figs, grapes and oranges. Maybe do a shot of tequila. Even tempt with a little belly dance. And exotically kiss the night away! . . .

2. Tell your honey you need to do a little exercise. Then grab him for a good kissing session. You'll both be feeling the post-workout high.

3. Next time you have a chocolate candy bar, don't fret about the calories (you'll burn them off while kissing!). Just consider the wonderful effects chocolate has when it comes to kissing. How bad can that be?

5
kama sutra kissing: exotic and erotic moves for puckering up

"Anything may take place at any time,
for love does not care for time or order."

VATSYANA (*KAMA SUTRA* PRE 6TH CENTURY)

 For the ultimate in passionate kissing, we turn to the *Kama Sutra*. Written in India sometime before the 6th century by Vatsyana (a Brahmin priest who was supposedly celibate), this sizzlin' self-

help love guide was so much more than a tantalizing rundown on the multiple ways to make boinga-boinga. It schooled young men in the singles scene, showing them how to decorate their bachelor pads, how to be well-versed in cultural subjects to chat up the ladies, and even how to groom themselves. You might say it was an ancient *Queer Eye for the Straight Guy*!

But did you know that the *Kama Sutra* is also one of the first kissing manuals? India was the kissing hotbed of the ancient East. And this love guide is filled with all sorts of juicy mouth-to-mouth techniques. While the *Kama Sutra* was intended for boys, you can be sure beautifully exotic Indian girls were reading this under their saris at night. They wanted to improve their kissing talents, too!

For more intimate and sensuous kissing that will be most admired, try these ancient yet hot as ever *Kama Sutra* kisses with a certain someone:

- *Throbbing Kiss*: "When a girl, setting aside her bashfulness a little, wishes to touch the lip that is pressed into her mouth, and with that object moves her lower lip, but not the upper one."

    * Focus on your honey's lower lip. Give all pleasure to that part of their mouth only. Don't be shy about it!

- *Touching Kiss*: "When a girl touches her lover's lip with her tongue, and having shut her eyes, places her hands on those of her lover."

    * When you come in to kiss your lovebug, gently sweep your tongue across his lips. And hold his hands. This is a very loving kiss.

- *Turned Kiss*: "When one of them turns up the face of the other by holding the head and chin, and the kissing."

    * With one hand, clasp your sweetie's hand in yours. With the other hand, gently take his chin. And turn it toward you for a kiss. Try this when you're in the mood to make the first move!

- *Pressed Kiss*: "When the lower lip is pressed with much force."

    * While kissing, just concentrate on the lower lip for a minute. The upper lip will cry

out, "Hey, what about me?" This kind of teasing makes for a little variety during some hot kissing.

- *Kiss of the Upper Lip*: "When a man kisses the upper lip of a woman, while she in return kisses his lower lip."

  * For some real sweet intimacy, get your cutie pie to kiss your bottom lip, and when he's doing that, kiss his upper lip. You'll look like happy fishes!

- *Clasping Kiss*: "When one of them takes both the lips of the other between his or her own."

  * During a deep, silky, sensual kiss, envelop your guy's lips with yours. This is super-duper intense kissing!

- *Fighting of the Tongue*: "When during the Clasping Kiss, if one of them touches the teeth, the tongue, and the palate of this other, with his or her tongue."

  * In the heat of it, take your lover's lips between yours. And thrust your tongue in their mouth. You might end up wrestling each other to the ground.

- *Kiss that Kindles Love*: "When a woman looks at the face of her lover while he is asleep, and kisses it to show her intention or desire."

  * When you find your pookie bear sound asleep, gently kiss their face (even if they're snoring!). They might not stir. But they'll dream of you and your kisses.

- *Kiss that Turns Away*: "When a woman kisses her lover while he is engaged in business, or while he is quarreling with her, or while he is looking at something else, so that his mind might be turned away."

  * If your man checks out some hottie across the room, don't stress it. Just grab his attention with one of your kisses. He'll be totally focused on you. And forget the hoochie. This move is also good during a disagreement. A silly spat will be replaced by cooing love whispers.

- *Kiss that Awakens*: "When a lover coming home late at night kisses his beloved who is asleep in her bed in order to show his desire."

  * If you find your lovebug fast asleep, pretend you're the Prince and he's Sleeping Beauty.

Kiss him gently but fully on the lips. This is sure to arouse him from a deep slumber.

With the *Kama Sutra*, your lips, mouth and tongue will transport the lucky recipient of your kisses to new heights. They'll all want to know your secret.

♡

6
what a guy wants

"A man snatches the first kiss, pleads for the second,
demands the third, takes the fourth, accepts the fifth—
and endures all the rest."

HELEN ROWLAND (1876-1950)

"A man's kiss is his signature."

MAE WEST (1892-1980)

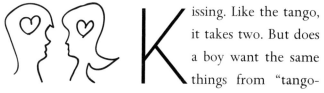 issing. Like the tango, it takes two. But does a boy want the same things from "tango-ing" we do? Does "tangoing" have the same effect on his head? His heart? Is it about the love for him? The ro-mance? Or the sex thing? Or is it some combination

of these in slightly different proportions to our own desires?

The quest for reaching a deeper understanding of the mysteries that are male have plagued fair ladies for centuries. It's an endless topic of exploration, stereotyping, generalization and controversy. Many an intelligent person has attempted to qualify and quantify the Venus and Mars, the Adam and Eve, and the ball and chain.

guy/girl differences

Thankfully, modern MRI technology has affirmed what we women have long intuited: There are actually structural differences between the male and female brains. Guys have more gray matter, so they tend to compartmentalize communication, use words to inspire action and zero in on the heart of things. We ladies are influenced by more white matter, which translates to being more verbal and emotional. Our corpus callosum, some whatsa-ma-ghiggy in the brain, is bigger. This explains the extraordinary female multitasking phenomenon, like filing our nails when having sex while remembering to take that blouse to the cleaners.

The differences are also about hormones and chromosomes. Guys pump and grunt testosterone while we surge and scream estrogen. They're strung with an X and Y chromosome, where we ladies have two Xs. Add

survey says...

How does a guy react if a girl kisses him while he's watching a game on TV?

a. Respond sweetly

b. Tell her to hold tight until halftime

c. Ignore her

d. Swat her with the remote

Most guys (82 percent) say they'd kiss you right back and then some. But it could also depend on the game. And how close it was 'til the end. So you could get the brush-off. Use your judgment, ladies. At least wait for commercial!

it all up, and it triggers the passionate sizzle and lusty kaboom of the battle of the sexes.

"Teach not thy lip such scorn, for it was made

For kissing, lady, not for such contempt."

WILLIAM SHAKESPEARE (*RICHARD III*)

so what *does* a guy want?

Yet none of this biology and physiology really explains the underpinning of what makes guys tick. What turns them on and off. Why they can't pick up their socks, put the toilet seat down or ask for directions. More important to us here and now, it doesn't explain what guys want when it comes to kissing.

Sure, we can succinctly elucidate what it is *we* want from this most pleasurable act. We'll analyze and theorize about our kissing with our gal pals 'til the cows come home. And we joke that all a guy seems to want from kissing (among other things) is for us to simply show up scantily clad in a bathing suit worthy of *Baywatch,* carrying nothing but a six-pack (okay, maybe a twelve-pack and a bag of pretzels). But is that really so? Do they have fewer needs when it comes to kissing? Do they

survey says...

Like us gals, guys remember their first kiss. So where did they learn about this life-altering, life-affirming maneuver?

a. Instructions from an older sibling

b. By practicing on a pillow or in a mirror

c. Kissing an older girl

d. Just "winged" it

e. Born with the talent

Half of the boys said they just "winged it." Did what came naturally. About one-third credit an "older woman" for their moves. Then there're those who believe they were born to kiss. Others admit to emulating that super-suave, secret agent man "Bond. James Bond." Nothing like kissing a James Bond.

desire and think about it less? Does it have less meaning? Or do they really just want beer and some salty snacks?

What if we were to discover that what a guy wants from kissing is really not that much different from what we want? It might be a narrow topic among the universal male/female dynamic to explore. Yet it's a significant one. Because truly understanding and embracing what a guy wants would likely lead to happier, sexier, more satisfying kissing. And isn't that what we want?

did you know ?

A man who kisses his lady good-bye when he leaves for work every morning averages a higher income than the guy who doesn't.

what a guy wants from kissing

"Now a soft kiss—Aye, by that kiss, I vow an endless bliss."

JOHN KEATS

In the male *Kissing* survey, a wide array of topics were covered: where and how guys liked to be kissed, what lights their fire and what snuffs out their candle. Whether a kiss always needs to lead to the bedroom. Whether kissing another when committed to someone is a no-no. Their responses were more similar to our own than you might expect. Maybe the great divide isn't as wide as we think.

PART I: A GUY'S THOUGHTS ON . . .

a kiss—does it have meaning?

Hands down, guys believe a kiss has full-bodied meaning. For them, it's a signal of what the future holds. An expression of love, happiness, intimacy, affection and even joy. It's the first physical sign of a connection, be it love or sex. A channeling of hormones. A start. The prelude to more fun.

"Every kiss is charged with something. Satisfaction.
Desire. Hope. Charm. A welcoming. Passion.
Every kiss has energy."

C . K .

"It tells us how much further the moment might go.
Is it casual, awkward or is it leading up to
something bigger/better?"

C . L .

"A kiss is more than just a peck. It means you've crossed a
certain line. A line she has allowed you to cross."

C . E .

"A kiss is not just a kiss, as someone once said. It
depends on who is doing the kissing! If it's a peck
on the cheek, it's a cocktail party or Aunt Sally. If it's
on the lips, it's sensual . . . And if it's on the lips

with a little more time and energy and tongue, well

then . . . that's something even better!"

D . S .

what attracts a guy to a girl?

- Her personality
- Her looks
- That certain something
- Something else

♡ **Looks might get their attention.** ♡
But character and personality win out!

Twenty-three percent said looks are the bait while 19 percent pointed to personality. But a combined majority of 60 percent are drawn to a mix of characteristics and traits, like her voice, her energy, the way she carries herself, her kindness to others, that certain sex and *je ne sais quoi* (fancy for "I don't know what").

"Looks. But personality has a big effect on looks. Plenty of

smoking girls get less smoking as you get to know them."

S . L .

"Physical attraction certainly counts, but I think it is the way she looks at me (Is there a smile? Is there a twinkle in the eyes?), acts with me (Do I get the occasional stroke of the hair and pat on the butt?), and acts toward me in company (Is she with me even though not next to me?)."

D . L .

"Her language. Not necessarily how she speaks, but the way she communicates. The way she moves. The way her face breaks into a smile. The way she applies lipstick. The way she dresses. All sorts of things."

C . D .

what makes a girl kissable?

- Sultry lips
- A certain vibe/come-hither look
- The possibility of sex
- Something else

♡ It's an aura. A look. That thing you can't define but feel. ♡

Forty-seven percent think it's about that vibe/look. Twenty-six percent think it's something else. Things romantic. Like love. And her eyes—*"There's a shining right before a kiss. There's a beaming."* And having fun together outside of sex.

Surprisingly, only 16 percent said the possibility of sex is what makes a girl *kissable*. However, they are strong believers that almost every action a guy takes when it comes to a girl is eventually about the sex thing.

And a combined 11 percent point to lips, look and possibility of sex.

what's sexier?—*kissing a girl who:*

- Looks like a top model but is short on brain power
- Has a great sense of humor and fetching way
- Dresses like a librarian but could be a real kitten
- Other

♡   Humor with soft, good energy is sexiest.   ♡

Humor came out on top, with 35 percent. Another 35 percent believe romantic qualities make a girl sexy— her tenderness, her vulnerability, her mystery, her responsiveness—*"The sexiest thing about a girl is a girl who wants to kiss back."*

Only 6 percent said they go for the model types. But 24 percent would be turned on by a Lois Lane librarian type who could be Supergirl in disguise.

PART II: KISSING MOODS AND ATTITUDES

"Don't have sex, man. It leads to kissing, and pretty soon you have to talk to them."

STEVE MARTIN

debunking stereotypes— is kissing just about sex?

It's long been a belief that guys aren't into kissing for the sake of kissing—that it's really just an appetizer for their main course. Where sometimes we girls just want an appetizer and no main course (and we always like a little coffee after dinner). Clearly a big generalization, but a long-standing notion nonetheless. So what did the fellas from *Kissing*'s survey have to say about this?

Fact or Fiction—Guys always want kissing to lead to sex

♥ **Not totally so!** ♥

Fifty-six percent said in the broad scheme that's not so. Yes, kissing should lead to sex at some point. But not every kiss needs to be consummated.

Forty-four percent said it's true. But age was a determining factor. Teens and twentysomething guys want kissing to lead to sex every time. The older they get, that connection is not necessarily made. A little kissing can be followed just as contentedly by sleep as by sex!

Fact or Fiction—Guys don't always seem to like to kiss much after sex

A roaring 75 percent said they *do* like to kiss after sex! (Hooray!) They also say they're just really, really tired. It's not that they don't want to coo, cuddle and kiss in that romantic, bonding way. They're just too pooped to pucker. So while the spirit be willing, the body be not able.

does kissing wane the longer a relationship lasts?

Well, it's a mixed bag.

For some, kissing remains a key part of the relationship—"*the gateway to communication.*"

"I think if she's a good kisser, you always want it!"

B. S.

"Fifteen years with the same girl, still love kissing. Me more than her."

D. K.

"Having been in a relationship for a long time, kissing has turned into something that says "you turn me on" and makes any encounter less routine. It's a big deal."

R. R.

"Kissing for me is the linchpin of intimacy, the cornerstone of communication. So if kissing fades, we're not communicating."

K. P.

For others, kissing can diminish over time. But it's recognized that kissing is something that should be safeguarded and cherished as a special thing.

> "It doesn't just fade for guys. Have a couple of kids, and you both begin to take on that "get in and out quick" approach toward, sex which establishes a bad precedent when kissing. This has to stop at all costs. Sex is GREAT! But nothing beats grabbing the person you love, pulling her close and laying one on her. That passes the vibe more than anything else."
>
> E . E .

> "Not that it's not fun to kiss as the relationship progresses, but it becomes more expected. The less expected stuff in a relationship, the better."
>
> C . K .

> "It can. Both people have to protect the fire."
>
> A . D .

> "Kinda true. In the early stages of a relationship, it's about getting to know her—the excitement of a new

> body, lips, exploring our bodies, ourselves. As the
> relationship matures, there's a comfort factor, and
> kissing episodes happen less."
>
> E . D .

so what puts a guy in the mood to kiss?

- A romantic setting, e.g., candles, soft music
- Good food and/or wine
- The possibility of sex
- Other stuff

♥ **Kissing might not just be about sex . . .** ♥
but it sure gets a boy's motor running!

After saying kissing isn't always about sex, 39 percent said the possibility of "*nuding up*" puts them in the mood to kiss. That's bit of a paradox! Maybe the operative word is *possibility.*

Thirty-three percent, though, were seduced by a bunch of feel good things. A wonderful dinner cooked at home. A smile. The look in her eyes. A girl's scent. Rainy days. Exercise. A relaxed mind. Intense and honest moments. And a combined 28 percent got that kissy feeling from a soft setting and nice vino. Hallelujah! Romance isn't dead yet!

and how does a guy feel about a girl making the first move?

We girls are often unsure about what to do here. The sexual revolution and feminist movement turned the tables. And there've been many a great chick book on this "Do you?" or "Don't you?" Some years it's okay. Other years, no way. So it's hard to know what's what. Do we take the chance? Get rejected? Appear like a floozy? Or do we sit back? Wait? And possibly lose out? Truth is, guys have their own trepidations. They might hold back, too—that fear of rejection thing, which we can all relate to.

So how does a guy feel if a gal were to kiss him first? To a degree, it remains a gray area:

Sixty-six percent said they like it when a girl seizes the opportunity—*"It's great when a woman expresses herself."*

But while the guys say they like a girl to make the move, 33 percent were only into this sometimes—*"It's all about how the move is made."*

So what's a girl to do with this?

Trust your instincts. But make sure his "kiss me" signal is as bright as the lights on a stadium JumboTron screen at night.

what about lipstick?—do guys prefer kissing girls with or without lipstick?

♡ **Keep 'em moist and natural, girls.** ♡

Seventy-five percent said without. Sure, some guys want a girl to have pouty red lips. But having moist, non-chapped natural lips was more important than "lipsticked" lips.

did you know ?

A lipstick imprint of a kiss made by Mick Jagger's mouth once sold for $1,600.

The 25 percent who said they'd kiss a girl with lipstick said it was okay for kissing to be a little messy sometimes. They also said lipstick is okay if she's the last person they'll see that night.

kissing and fidelity

In our world today, it's hard to know what's considered permissible or not. Celebrities, politicians and athletes have redrawn the lines. And peoples' attitudes seem to have changed—or have they?

Here's what the guys had to say:

DO THEY CONSIDER KISSING CHEATING?

A resounding 68 percent said yes. Anything you'd do with another girl that you wouldn't do in front of your girl is cheating.

Twenty-one percent said it depends on the situation and parties involved. Intertwined tongues would be over the line, but a friendly kiss on the lips not.

Have they ever kissed a friend's girlfriend or significant other?

Fifty-three percent said no. They might have thought about it, but didn't. Three percent came close.

Forty-four percent said yes. Situations like a roommate with a girlfriend who boldly crawled into bed made it hard to resist. And alcohol was usually involved. Tequila can provoke wild craziness!

What would they do if their girl kissed another guy?

- Break up with her
- Forgive her
- Kiss another girl for revenge
- Try to make her happy so she doesn't do it again

♡   Could be curtains. But they'll hear you out.   ♡

The guys were pretty tough here. Forty-six percent said they'd end it. But they'd also want to know what the circumstance was.

Twenty-three percent would be forgiving. They recognize they might have done something that led to it.

Only 8 percent said they'd kiss another girl out of spite, while the other 23 percent would remember to bring flowers and compliment her more often.

PART III:
HOW AND WHERE TO KISS HIM

"A legal kiss is never as good as a stolen one."

GUY DE MAUPASSANT (1850-1893)

Let's start with the basics.

how does a guy like to be kissed?

- Deep and passionately
- Slow and gently
- With tongue
- A combination of the above

♡   **Kiss 'em every which way!**   ♡

99.999 percent want the combo kissing platter—all of the above. Each has their place at the table. The key is to try a few things on the menu and create your own magic meal.

where does a guy want your hands when you're kissing him?

- Around his body
- Below the waist
- Running through his hair
- Stroking his face and neck

♡ **Touch him here, there and everywhere!** ♡
Just touch him!

We all know good kissing isn't just about contact with the mouth, lips and tongue. While kissing, boys pretty much want your hands anywhere and everywhere. It almost doesn't matter, as long as you're caressing them somewhere!

Specifically, 33 percent like a girl's hands around their body. Another 33 percent like to have their face and neck stroked. Twenty percent want your hands in their hair. And 14 percent want you coasting below their shoreline (surely that percentage should be higher!). Most of all, just stay close. And do what comes naturally.

so, what's a kissing turn-on?

Again, guys aren't so particular. They simply like the action of kissing. It's all good for them.

And what they want is really not that much different than what we want:

- Softness, warmth and tenderness
- Passion and enthusiasm, even a little force
- Moist, strong lips on all parts of the body— lips shouldn't be flimsy or noncommittal
- A tongue that knows just how much and how little
- Lip sucking—lower and upper, please!
- Physical closeness—not grinding, but intertwining
- Good smells and tastes
- Deep eye contact
- Smiles and laughter

what can kill a kiss?

What puts the kibosh on it for them is pretty much what does it for us:

- Bad breath, dryness, unpleasant taste, a slip of some gas
- No passion or fun
- Chewing gum, smoking, chewing tobacco
- A crying baby or ringing telephone or door-bell
- Biting—a little nip is okay, but be careful
- An overly active, crazy, deep tongue or a tongue that "*licks like a zoo animal*"
- Bad attitude, negative disposition
- Stiff, wooden lips—overall rigidity
- When she doesn't want to kiss you but you're still trying!

♡ **Anything yucky.** ♡

where does a guy like to kiss?

Like us, guys want to kiss anywhere that's comfortable. So the couch and bed are favorites with them, too.

Other good kissing spots include:

- Outdoors/in nature—the beach, under the stars or on a blanket in a grassy field

- Street corner—very romantic and spontaneous
- Under an umbrella on a rainy day
- On the dance floor—it's nice to lose yourself
- On the water—in a boat or swimming pool
- The shower—and shower kissing usually leads to other pleasant activities!

> "Kisses are the remnants of paradise."
> JOSEPH CONRAD (1857-1924)

where on his body does a guy liked to be kissed?

Again, like us gals, boys want to be kissed anywhere and everywhere. Apart from the lips, they like kisses to the:

- Neck, ears and shoulders
- Stomach and chest, and anywhere around the abdomen is very sensual. A little nibble to the hip is nice, too
- Places between their legs (oh my!)

♡ Anywhere and everywhere.
He just likes it when you kiss him! ♡

*where a guy likes to
kiss a girl on her body:*

Along with her lips, a guy enjoys kissing a girl's:

- Face, back of the neck, ears and beyond
- Breasts and stomach
- Inner thighs (my oh my!)
- Sternum and back
- Ankles and back of knees

"A kiss of the mouth often touches not the heart."

H. S. BOHN

(*HANDBOOK OF PROVERBS*, 1796-1884)

*what about wild 'n crazy kisses?
what does a guy like?*

Apart from maybe trying a little honey on the lips or the
Spider-Man upside-down kiss, guys seem to just appre-

ciate good ol' fashioned, unadulterated kissing. Nothing too freaky. Maybe melted chocolate. Sharing a mint. Or a kissing game like "I dare you . . ." Otherwise, follow the K.I.S.S. rule—Keep It Simple Sweetie. And mean it.

> "There is always one who kisses
> and one who allows the kiss."
>
> GEORGE BERNARD SHAW
>
> (*MAN AND SUPERMAN*, 1856-1950)

so, do guys have kissing fantasies?

Sure. Their lusty minds wander just like ours do. Here's who they'd like to kiss:

Hot and Sultry	Fresh-Faced	Exotic and Mysterious
Angelina Jolie	Diane Lane	Naomi Campbell
Jennifer Lopez	Scarlett Johannsen	Juliette Binoche
Vanessa Marcil	Christy Turlington	Lucy Liu
Halle Berry	Jessica Simpson	Salma Hayek
Charlize Theron	Elisha Cuthbert	Rosario Dawson
	Ashley Judd	

PART IV: GUYS' MOST MEMORABLE KISSES

"I kissed my first girl and smoked my first cigarette

on the same day. I haven't had time for

tobacco ever since."

ARTURO TOSCANINI (1867-1957)

And like us, guys remember those exceptional kisses. They have their own scrapbook of sentimental memories.

on their first kiss

"You should not take a fellow of eight years old and

make him swear to never kiss the girls."

ROBERT BROWNING

(*FRA LIPPO LIPPI*, 1855)

Most of the guys had their first kiss somewhere between the ages of five and thirteen, and they remember this moment in charming detail.

"Her name was Kate. It was seventh grade.

And I had to stand on a chair to kiss her."

E. H.

"I was about six years old and at a neighbor's birthday
party. I handed over my gift to the birthday girl, who
tried to plant one on me as a thank you, but I ran
and hid under a table. Eventually she caught up to
me and the kiss was very wet and very icky."

C . V .

"I was thirteen, and it was with a girl who lived next
door to us. We were all just hanging around the
neighborhood, and she pulled me into her backyard.
I was frightened at first because I had no idea what
I was doing. Then I was scared her father was
going to come out and catch us."

B . D .

Some of our favorite male celebrities' first kisses were
just as clumsy and humorous. Even achingly anguished!

"It was the most disgusting thing in my whole life.
The girl injected about a pound of saliva into my mouth,
and when I walked away, I had to spit it out."

LEONARDO DICAPRIO

"I was in the fourth grade. We made a plan to meet
in her garage and kiss. It was like this business deal. I go
right up to her, kiss her. Then I ran home."

BRAD PITT

"I was about fifteen and met her at a party. I suggested
we meet at a park the next day. We held hands,
and there was a little kissing and sort of fumbling.
But once that happened, I didn't really know
what to do next. It was a very clumsy affair."

STING

most memorable kiss

"We sat and kissed and kissed until our lips were bloody.
I could have gone on kissing her for a year."

RYAN O'NEAL ON HIS FIRST DATE

WITH FARRAH FAWCETT

From risky/friskiness to sentimental ones, the gentlemen of the *Kissing* survey have their special memories, too. Romance is alive and well in the heart of a male!

"My most memorable kiss took place with the woman who would eventually become my wife. We boarded a train and remained lip-locked pretty much the entire way. It was very wet but not at all icky. We could have been held up at gunpoint and it wouldn't have mattered. We had been lost in each other all day."

C . V .

"Well, meeting my recent girlfriend . . . I approached her at a bar, we spoke for a few minutes, and then I went for it. I couldn't resist her lips. . . ."

W . W .

"The first time I kissed my wife. Sounds corny, but true. Wasn't a great kiss. She couldn't stop smiling, so I got a lot of teeth."

D . K .

"Wedding day. In front of all those people. It wasn't
perfunctory but rather 'I really love this woman.' "

C . F .

most embarrassing kiss

"Everyone winds up kissing the wrong person good night."

A N D Y   W A R H O L   (1 9 2 8 - 1 9 8 7)

Ah, we all want to cringe when we think of certain kisses.
Even guys have had those "Argh, I can't believe I did
that!!!" moments that can turn you shades of red.

"One night after a company baseball outing, I made out
with a co-worker at an after party. I thought we were in a
secluded area. Turns out the ENTIRE company saw it. . . ."

T . D .

"When I had braces, I kissed a girl who also had
braces. We didn't do the mythical "braces lock" but
did bump metal pretty hard. I remember we laughed
at the time, but thinking 'that hurt.' "

A . M .

"With my wife. I think I burped midkiss, gave
her a shot of beer breath."

N. C.

"A friend's stepmother gave me a slip of the tongue.
I remember being shocked . . . but I liked it."

H. N.

KISSING ACROSS THE GENDER GAP

It seems we're not the only ones filled with oooey-gooey feel-good when it comes to kissing. It can be just as lovely a thing for a guy as a girl. Like us gals, guys want to connect in that meaningful way, be shown how special they are, and feel sexy and desired. While those scans show our brains are structured differently, our hearts apparently are made up of similar parts.

Kissing is just as much pressure for a man as it is for a woman. Many thoughts can go whippin' and zippin' through their heads midkiss. Is their saliva under control? Their tongue? Is that 5 o'clock shadow chaffing? Are they mixing it up with enough variety? Impressing did you know ?

In Italy, there's an armor-clad statue of a sixteenth-century soldier named Guidarello Guidarelli. And tradition has it that a girl who kisses the statue will marry within one year. Ladies have been lining up around the block for years waiting for their turn to plant one in hopes of getting them a husband.

us with their know-how? And leaving us wanting more? It's a lot to think about when trying to be suave and romantic while concentrating on the pleasure being given and received.

WHAT A GUY WILL DO WHEN INSPIRED BY A KISS

- 1631: The Indian Emperor Shad Jahan built the Taj Mahal in honor of his wife. It would take over twenty years and twenty thousand workers to complete, and would stand as one of the eight wonders of the world. She must have been some kisser!

- 1796: The French warrior Napoleon longed for his wife Josephine's kisses so badly that during war on the battle-fronts, he repeatedly dispatched couriers with his romantic missives. So what if he was risking their lives. His girl had to know! Here's a taste of his hot-hot letters:

> *"Some fine night the doors will open, and I'll be . . . I hope before long to crush you with a million kisses burning as though beneath the equator."*

> *"A kiss on the heart, another one a little lower, another lower still, far lower."*

- 1886: Frenchman Francois August Rodin sculpted *The Kiss*. It remains one of the most romantic pieces of art in the Western world.

daily kisses XOXO

1. If there's a guy you want to kiss—*carpe diem*! Men are into self-expression.

2. On that first kiss with a new guy, make it passionate. And make it sensual. But don't get too creative (licking his cheeks and lips is not sexy right out of the box). Or overeager (watch the tongue probing). Easy does it all the time. Always leave him wanting more.

   "My child, if you finally decide to let a man kiss you, put your whole heart into it. No man likes to kiss a rock."
   LADY CHESTERFIELD (1600S)

3. Be spontaneous with your kisses. Next time you're out for a romantic dinner, touch his arm or thigh a couple of times. Then coyly apologize, saying something like, "I'm sorry, my hand must have slipped." And as you wait for dessert, lean in kiss him softly and say, "I couldn't wait a minute longer for something sweet."

7
how to be
irresistibly kissable

"Why does a man take for granted that a girl who flirts
with him wants him to kiss her—when nine times out of
ten, she only wants him to want to kiss her?"

HELEN ROWLAND (1876-1950)

With all this insight on what a guy wants from a kiss, what should a girl do if she wants to *get* kissed?

tips for getting kissed

Well, there's always the vixenish "come-hither-kiss-me" moves, like the twirling of the hair, and licking of the lips, or the more coquettish things like the throwing back of the head in lilting laughter, and the Betty Boop batting of the eyelashes. There's even the classic "girl punch" to a boy's arm as we feign with a giggle, "Ssssttttooooop it!"

Here are some practical body-speak tips that say "Kiss me now. Kiss me well. And kiss me deep and long." Do these, and you'll be sure to get a reaction:

1. *Smile*: This is one of the best ways to engage a guy (and hopefully get him to kiss you). It tells him you're friendly, positive, happy and in a good mood—all the things a guy will want to know before approaching you. It also shows off your *kiss-a-luscious* lips and pearly whites. You know he'll be checking those out. So flash a smile!

2. *Be Welcoming*: Use your body to broadcast that you're "open for kissing." If you're at a party or bar or places where there are cute guys you'd like to smooch, stand with your arms to the side. Or place one hand on your hip if you're feeling jaunty. Your charm and allure will be impossible to resist.

3. *Use Your Eyes*: They say the eyes are the windows to the soul. The eyes are also the little "kiss me" flags. Look directly into his baby blues (or baby browns), and wave your banner. It communicates self-confidence and interest, and it's hard to ignore. A word of caution—too much eyeballin' can come off a tad like a wiggy kitty. So just like with everything else, exercise moderation.

4. *Give a Little Nod*: If you're talking with a guy and feel the *fuego*, give a little nod or tilt of the head as he regales you with his sports victories or business dealings. It shows a nice level of interest and attention on your part. Which translates to him— "she wants me to kiss her." Just as mighty gladiators lived or died by a nod, so, too, can a kiss be born or never take flight.

5. *Skooch in A Little Closer*: Assuming you're standing or seated next to your object of desired affection, move closer. Lean in. Tilt your head toward him. This creates a cozy, intimate feeling. It's just the two of you. By giving him your total attention, he will do the same for you. It will also confirm his instincts. If he's been thinking "I wanna kiss her," he now knows you wanna, too.

6. *Get a Little Touchy/Feely*: In this age of political correctness, we tend to be much more careful about touching someone. Yet that doesn't mean we can't use touch when appropriate. Like when snuggled into a comfy booth, listening to some nice piano bar music in an after-hours club. The evening has been high class. You're hoping it's gonna end in a kiss. So reach out. Gently touch his arm or his hand. Maybe even put your hand on his leg if you're feeling like a bobcat. And watch how your signal is received.

♡

8
kissing around
the world

"Kisses are the messengers of love."

DANISH PROVERB

"Lovers can live on kisses and cool water."

OLD FRENCH PROVERB

Kissing. According to anthropologists, over 90 percent of the world's population kisses. It's one of those things threading through us, like laughing, making whoopee and sending email that's as essential to life as breathing, water and food.

So given the universal appeal of this most delightful demonstration of love and affection, wouldn't you be surprised to know there are some people who don't kiss the way we do, or even kiss at all? That there are different canoodling customs that vary from country to country? Or that in this day and age, puckering in public is seriously frowned upon, and even against the law in some places?

To get a better understanding of cultural attitudes and mores around the world today, we need to look at what was going on yesterday.

"sniffing" vs. kissing

That randy ol' evolutionary chap Charles Darwin believed kissing was natural—an innate part of foreplay, like caressing, nuzzling, stroking and other sexy, feel-good love moves. But Darwin also observed that not all cultures kissed. Even in the nineteenth century, some still rubbed noses. And it wasn't just the Eskimos. There were tribes in faraway Pacific places that did, too.

"Two would greet each other in the traditional
manner by rubbing noses together."

ASEN BALIKCI IN
THE NETSILIK ESKIMO (1970)

More accurately, Darwin noted these natives were sniffing one another's cheeks, nose and neck to pick up the scent of their unique oils—a kind of sequel to the caveman's breath kiss back in Bedrock. While that

did you know ?

It's believed the ancient Egyptians were nose-rubbing sniff kissers too. Despite numerous records of antiquity detailing everything from embalming to making beer and wine, there's no mention of kissing. So the people of the mighty pyramids either didn't think lip-locking was important enough to write about, or didn't do it.

might sound odd by our standards of deodorants, perfumed soaps and air-fresheners, taking in a deep whiff of someone's personal eau de toilette was how people recognized family and friends. You can just imagine the social commentary at cocktail luaus—"Hello. How are you? Have we met before?" Sniff. Sniff. "Yes, I remember you now." This affectionate olfactory action could be dubbed the "sniff kiss."

how kissing spread around the world

While some early cultures were sniff kissing, others were lip kissing. Ancient India is credited for evolving kissing to the marvelous mouth caress we relish today. They were also the first to write about it. In Sanskrit texts from 1500 B.C., we see words like *sniff*, *touch* and *lick* when referring to the mouth. By 1200 B.C., sensual passages describe lovers as "setting mouth to mouth" and "drinking the moisture of lips."

"She set her mouth to my mouth and made a
noise that produced pleasure in me."

FROM THE EPIC POEM *MAHABHARATA*

(INDIA, CIRCA 1000 B.C.)

If the old East created the style and technique of sensuous smooching, the ancient West would popularize it.

When that Greek warrior Alexander the Great invaded India in 326 B.C., he discovered the pleasure of puckering up. Taking this sexy act with him to Persia and elsewhere in the Middle East as well as back home in Greece, kissing snapped, crackled and popped  through the Mediterranean like wildfire through a parched forest.

"Give me another naughty kiss before we part."

PLAUTUS

Kissing in this vibrant golden era was pagan, lusty and bawdy. Everyone was kissing everyone and everything (think decadent orgies and rowdy toga parties). And the armies of Greece and Rome made it their mission to spread this delightful activity wherever they went, conquering Africa and Europe with a sword and a kiss.

Not surprisingly, the uninhibited kissing of B.C. would hit a wall. By the early second and third centuries A.D., juicy canoodling would be considered evil. Lawmakers decreed all sorts of crazy things, like kissing must be passionless, that it could only occur after supper and that those who "bussed" too ardently would be branded adulterers. Even holding hands was considered a major no-no.

By the Middle Ages, social kissing remained pretty discreet, but things began to lighten up. Refined lip-

did you know ?

The ancient Romans were the first to develop a vocabulary of words defining different kinds of kisses. There was *Osculum*— the standard "hello" kiss between couples or friends; *Basium*—the passionate kiss typical of spontaneous smooching between two lovers; and *Savium*, the deep tongue kissing.

locking was now acceptable, even a mark of gentility. Knights in shining armor who trained in jousting and fencing also learned how to perfect their pucker. Then before you knew it, kissing reached a frenzied pitch again, only to be squelched by laws that made it a crime for unmarried people to kiss, and the plague (that will do it every time!).

By the fifteenth and sixteenth centuries, social kissing would be replaced with a simple bow, proper curtsy or topping of the hat. This was also around the time when explorers like Marco Polo and Sir Francis Drake sailed east, where they tried to introduce lip-locking to sniff-kissing natives.

But the Western tongue tango didn't go over well in Asia and the Pacific. Taboos and misconceptions limited the mouth to eating and talking, not necking. They actually considered kissing kind of frightful—that it could suck the spirit out of their body or allow evil in. So much for a delectable little smooch between a guy and girl!

Even today, there are locales that are not completely keen on kissing as we think of it. Furthermore, there are rules and customs in various corners of the globe that differ from our own puckering protocol.

"Look at these people!

They suck each other's saliva and dirt!"

TSONGA PEOPLE OF SOUTHERN AFRICA

ON THE EUROPEAN PRACTICE OF KISSING

(1927)

kissing etiquette around the world today

For the most part, kissing is the worldwide way people say hello, express their love and affection or show respect and homage to another.

But going from country to country, between cultural habits and changing times, customs vary. Some places are big fans of kissing while others don't even allow it. And where kissing was once taboo, throngs of lovers now meet to pucker simultaneously in celebration. Whatever it might be, kissing continues to be one of the few things that doesn't require translation. It can be the beginning of a wonderful conversation. Even if you don't speak the language.

WHERE KISSING IS HOT

"Kisses are the language of love, so let's talk it over."
AMERICAN PROVERB

As it was historically, Westerners, especially Americans, are the most enamored with necking, even preoccupied with it. Just open a magazine, turn on the tube or catch a movie. Kissing practically stands out as a topic of greater import than most world events. People in the East and elsewhere might view us as shamelessly kiss-obsessed. And we are. Smooching a playful boy from the U.S. of A. is as American as apple pie and Chevrolet.

But when it comes to social graces, Europe is the kissing capital of the world. Men kiss women. Women kiss women. Men kiss men. And puckering in public is par for the European course. Everyone says hello with at least two kisses—one for each cheek. And kissing is not just for family and social situations; some Europeans even kiss in the workplace.

Here's a rundown by country to help you in your kissing travels across the continent, contributed in part by some research done by the folks at Blistex:

france

The French have always been big kissers. Many think they invented French kissing, but in fact, they didn't. The term is slang for deep kissing made trendy by Americans in 1923. At the time, the French were viewed as shockingly oversexed. Ironically, the French don't refer to a kiss with tongue as a "French kiss." They call it a "tongue kiss" or "soul kiss."

As for social situations, multiple kisses are standard in France. Usually one for each cheek (a practice that started in the 1600s to avoid any misinterpretation). And you kiss anyone anywhere—for a quick drink with friends, at a business meeting even with people who've only just met. The kissing always starts on the right cheek. And while most stick with two kisses, some places in France go for four. In others, three. The chic beaches in the south like St. Tropez get carried away with five or six.

did you know ?

The Maraichins in France's Britanny region have perfected a single kiss that lasts for hours. What powerful puckers!

On a side note, in France, kissing only one cheek implies romantic interest. So be careful!

italy

Italians mostly reserve kisses for family and close friends. There are no rules on how many or which cheek to start with. For casual encounters, hugs and handshakes are acceptable.

netherlands

Kissing here always begins and ends on the same cheek, so three kisses are standard. When greeting a family member or elderly person, toss in a few more in a show of respect and affection.

switzerland

The land of chocolate and precision watches is a three-kiss country, too.

united kingdom

As Brits tend to be a wee shy and reserved, "snogs" are given mainly to family and friends. For others, a handshake or a nod is perfectly fine. Even just a friendly "hello" works. More and more, though, Brits are beginning to kiss beyond their inner circles.

> "If we want to hug or kiss, we always do that in
> private. Other people have other things,
> but this is just a fact of life for us now."
> DUCHESS OF YORK ON
> KISSING THE DUKE OF YORK

belgium

The number of kisses depends on the age of the person you're kissing. For someone around your age—one kiss. For someone older than you, three. But they must be at least ten years older, so judge carefully!

spain, austria and scandinavia

These are two-kiss countries. And in Spain, start with the right cheek.

"A kiss without a mustache is like an egg without salt."
SPANISH PROVERB

germany

There's more handshaking than kissing here. Kissing is usually reserved for family and close friends.

"No one can forbid an honorable kiss."
GERMAN PROVERB

> "He's (my boyfriend) promised to kiss me
> on the other side of the (Berlin) wall."
>
> BRITTA KIEHEN, AGE 19

Europeans aren't the only big puckerers. There are other places where kissing is passionately embraced and celebrated socially and romantically.

philippines

The Philippines are in love with the notion of a kiss. So much so they rejoice with festivals called "Lovapaloozas."

did you know ?

Sweden is big on promoting good dental hygiene. So much so that their largest pharmacy chain, *Apoteket*, is calling on volunteers to smooch their way into the record books for the longest lip-lock. The couple selected will get a kissing coach and tips on flossing and better brushing. Now that's public service at its best.

On Valentine's Day, thousands of Philippino couples kiss at midnight across different cities, led by their respective mayor and his wife amid strains of "What the World Needs Now Is Love" while fireworks flare.

australia

Kissing is very popular Down Under. And in different cities, lip-locking can vary in style and meaning. In Sydney, kisses are often a come-on to sex, whereas in Brisbane they're more mellow, even a little sloppy.

did you know ?

Thailand is a place for adventurous smooching. Every Valentine's Day, engaged couples from around the world celebrate their big day by exchanging vows, rings and kissing underwater off the coast of the southern Trang province. That's serious lung power!

russia

Kissing has always been held in great regard here. Back in the day, a kiss from the tsar was the highest sign of recognition. Today, some dramatically describe a Russian kiss as a "very long and passionate kiss without spit or snot." Such a kiss is believed to make your head spin to the point where you fall down dizzy. But most Russians think their necking is no different from any other nationalities.

> ". . . strong, unexpected, from the bottom of the heart."
>
> LEONID BRESHNEV, FORMER
> SOVIET LEADER ON AN EXAMPLE
> OF A RUSSIAN KISS

brazil

There's lots of kissing and hugging in this hot climate! Coming and going, men kiss women. Women kiss women. And men hug each other. It's a very passionate, intimate society that's keen on expression. Ladies even have a variation on the kiss—when greeting each other, they put their cheeks together and kiss the air (not to be confused with the superficial "air kiss" out of Beverly Hills and other swanky zip codes where ladies lunch).

WHERE KISSING IS A BIG NO-NO

"Rules against kissing exist because
Malaysians are a prudish lot."
MAT SAAT ZAKI, PSYCHOLOGIST,
NATIONAL UNIVERSITY OF MALAYSIA

Surprisingly, there are places today where kissing is not done socially (or at all!). And PDA is forbidden. Religious and cultural mores have a lot to do with it. Here's a rundown:

indonesia

Believe it or not, in February, 2005, the government proposed a ban on PDA between unmarried couples.

Violators could risk 10 years in jail and fines of up to $42,590.

In protest of this pending law, teenagers staged a kissing festival near Bali at an annual event known as the Med-Medan. As tradition goes, kissing was used to ward of bad luck. So teens took turns praying and puckering-up to celebrate this ritual in praise of kissing. That's teen spirit!

malaysia

Couples here can be fined up to $75 for kissing. Courts charge lovers with "indecent behavior" just for snogging in the park. So much for a romantic stroll after dinner!

india and pakistan

Kissing in public is not permitted. It's even censored on TV shows coming from the West, and movies made in these countries feature lots of dancing but no smooching.

"In India, kissing is just not done."
MIRA NAIR, FILM DIRECTOR

As things go in modern times though, some couples are kissing in public (even if they might find themselves in prison!), and flashes of kissing are starting to appear in films.

turkey

While there is no law against kissing in public, PDA is considered an offense. Words like *kiss* and *love* are prohibited by the state telephone company for use on pocket-pagers. So much for wireless winkin' ;)!

But kissing socially is seen as a sign of respect, especially when greeting an elder. It's custom to kiss their hand and then bring that hand to your forehead.

> "When we were visiting one village, an elderly man came up to me and wanted to kiss my hand. I got a bit angry and said, 'You are older than I am. I should kiss your hand.' But he replied, 'I am not kissing your hand. I am kissing the hand of our struggle.'"
>
> LEYLA ZANA, TURKISH POLITICIAN

the himalayas

People from Nepal don't kiss at all. It's always been taboo. For them, the mouth and saliva are dirty. So there's no puckering up of any kind.

WHERE TIMES ARE CHANGING . . .

"When I met people here (in the United States), it was kissing and hugging. In Japan, you just bow."

SEIKO, AGE TWENTY-FOUR,
JAPANESE SUPERSTAR SINGER

Asia has a complicated relationship with kissing. Countries there that centuries ago wrote treaties on the art of love would later view kissing as a vulgar social offense and terrible taboo. But more and more, Asians are warming up to it again. Even kissing in public. Be it generational or as a backlash, the ways of the West are filtering in through MTV and *Sex and the City* DVD's.

japan

Paradoxically, the land of geishas and public baths is prudish on kissing. While Japanese might canoodle in the privacy of their home, socially, they bow or shake hands. In the first half of the 20th century, there was even a law that declared kissing as something that was "dirty, vulgar, undignified and spread disease." They also used to edit the kissing scenes out of American movies that came East.

Today, a kissing movement is afoot. Japanese teens pucker up in public more and more. This is pretty shocking for a conservative culture. But the younger generation has made PDA a popular activity. They've even

did you know ?

In the 1920s, when August Rodin's famous sculpture *The Kiss* went on display in a Tokyo museum, it created such a controversy that the statue was put behind a bamboo curtain.

named it—*hito mae kisu*. Of course the older generation is scandalized and hopes this fad will fade.

china

Ironically, the first Asian country that allowed kissing in the movies (*Two Women in the House*, 1926) would come to consider kissing inappropriate. A 1990 article in the *Beijing Workers' Daily* warned lip-locking was unhealthy— "a harmful form of behavior." Kissing between adults, even adults and children, was discouraged. So most of China just says hello or shakes hands when greeting.

> "Husbands only think of themselves,
> and so there's no kissing or hugging."
> LIU DALIN, PRESIDENT OF THE SHANGHAI
> SEX EDUCATION RESEARCH SOCIETY

But like Japan, a new generation of Chinese are embracing the kiss, so much so that contests are being organized to encourage it, like the French-kissing event sponsored by an appliance store in the Jiangsu province. Lovers lined up in hopes of winning generous prize money. This caused great dismay among the older population, who have called on authorities to prevent further contests!

south korea

Overt physical contact with the opposite sex is not common. On the flip side, it's not unusual for people of the same sex to walk hand in hand. For the most part, social interaction consists of a handshake. But like Japan and China, kissing is being influenced by the West, and necking has caught on here, too.

> "Fifteen years ago, there was not even kissing in
> Korean films. But now . . . whoa!"
>
> SANG KU JOO, FORMER KOREAN SOLDIER

kissing in other languages

In case you happen to be traveling abroad, here's a quick kissing dictionary.

Italian	*bacio, pomiciare*
German	*kusse, schmusen*
Hebrew	*na`shikah*
Armenian	*bacheeg*
Greek	*filie*
Russian	*potselui*
Hindu	*chummi*
Spanish	*beso*
French	*un baiser, embrasse-moi (kiss me)*
Korean	*boh-boh*
Burmese	*hmuay-hmuay*

WORLDWIDE
KISSING RECORDS

- Longest Underwater Kiss: April 2nd, 1980. Tokyo, Japan. Two minutes, eighteen seconds.
- Longest Kiss: February 14th, 2004. Vincenza, Italy (that's literally where Romeo and Juliet were from). Thirty-one hours and eighteen minutes. The man needed oxygen afterward (that girl literally sucked the breath from his body!).

- Most People Kissing at Once: February 14th, 2004. Philippines. Five thousand three hundred couples smooched simultaneously, breaking the previous record held in Chile (4,445 couples).

daily kisses XOXO

1. Throw an international party and play "Kissing 'Round the World." Everyone draws the name of a country from a hat and acts out the rules of kissing etiquette with whomever they fancy. Some lucky partygoers will get lip. Others only a hand-shake. Or a bow. Some will be banned with no kissing at all!

2. Keep mistletoe up year 'round. Why should kissing under a pretty sprig be left for the holidays only? Better yet, carry it in your bag so you always have an occasion to kiss.

3. Pretend you live in ancient Roman times and kiss everyone you meet with passion and gusto. Kiss their rings, too, while you're at it!

♡

9
kissing folklore and superstitions

"There is a stone that whoever kisses,

Oh! He never misses to grow eloquent.

'Tis he may clamber to a lady's chamber,

Or become a member of parliament."

FRANCIS SYLVESTER MAHONY ON

KISSING THE BLARNEY STONE (1804-1866)

fun customs and beliefs

There are some charming European legends dating way back that are just as familiar today.

kissing the blarney stone

The Blarney Stone is located in Ireland at the fifteenth-century Blarney Castle in Cork. It's believed those who kiss the Blarney Stone are bestowed with the gift of eloquence and good luck. The stone is set in the wall below the battlements, so to kiss it is not such an easy task. It requires leaning over backward while holding the parapet railing.

It's reputed the stone was mentioned in the Bible as "Jacob's Pillow," and brought to Ireland during the Crusades. Another tale has the stone given by an old woman who was saved from drowning by a man named McCarthy. The lady, who turned out to be a witch, told McCarthy the secret of the stone as a reward. She claimed it would give him the gift of eloquence in return for a kiss.

The term *blarney* was introduced by Queen Elizabeth I. It means "pleasant talk, intending to deceive without offending."

"Kiss me, I'm Irish!"
IRISH SAYING

kissing under the mistletoe

While the roots of this custom are unknown, this flirty tradition likely began in Roman times with the festival of Saturnalia. It's also associated with the Druids and Scandinavians as a sign of peace and fertility.

The etiquette of mistletoe kissing varies. A smooch can be given to anyone who passes under it. Later versions required a man to pluck the berry when he kissed a lady. When there're no more berries on the sprig, there'll be no more kissing! And to refuse a kiss will bring bad luck.

kiss the boo boo

Believing a kiss held magic powers (that it does!), the English would kiss a hurt finger to heal it. It was also thought to be the cure-all for infant injuries. Kisses always make things better!

a kiss for luck

The French started kissing playing cards for luck while gambling. Some people still kiss a pair of dice before rolling.

st. agnes day, january 21st

It's believed if a single girl does not kiss on this day, she will soon find true love! This tradition dates back to the fourth century and a young woman named Agnes, who was executed for refusing to enter a prearranged marriage knowing she'd have to kiss her husband (harsh!).

There are also a bunch of signs that forecast a kiss is imminent or that require a kiss to ward off any possible bad karma:

If	It Means
Your nose itches . . .	You'll be kissed by a fool.
A standing man bends over and kisses a pretty woman . . .	They will soon quarrel.
A bride doesn't cry after the groom kisses her at the altar . . .	Their marriage will not be happy.
The first woman a man sees in the morning is an old woman . . .	He will have bad luck all day unless he kisses her.
You are caught in the open during a thunderstorm, cross your heart and then kiss the ground 3 times . . .	You will be protected from a lightning strike.
You have a toothache, kiss a donkey on the nose . . .	Your toothache will go away.

Just for good measure, you should probably kiss someone if you walk under a ladder, see a black cat or crack a mirror. While you're at it, smooch someone after you throw salt over your shoulder. Or even when you knock on wood. And make every Friday the Thirteenth a national "Give A Kiss" day!

♡

10
a few more reasons
to love a good kiss

"And from this slumber you shall wake

when true love's kiss the spell shall break."

SLEEPING BEAUTY (DISNEY, 1959)

Kissing. From a very young age, we learn to associate it with the deliciousness of romance. It's right there in our favorite childhood storybooks:

- Princess lays in a spellbound slumber . . . is kissed by a handsome prince . . . and awakens happily ever after!

- Princess withers away, locked in a dark tower . . . is rescued with a kiss by a handsome prince . . . and rides away tickled pink!
- Princess scrubs floors in indentured servitude . . . is kissed by a handsome prince who fits her with a snappy pair of glass slippers . . . and, you guessed it, acquires a closet full of stylish pumps, slingbacks and sandals Carrie Bradshaw would covet!

In our adult lives, though, we learn kissing is so much more than the fantasy of our bedtime stories. Sure, we still like to primp and preen like a princess and feel pretty in our dresses, but romance is much more complicated than those fairy tales. Sometimes kissing doesn't come easily. Sometimes our partners don't give us the attention we need.

And sometimes we might do crazy things in the name of a kiss. Whether we care to admit it, the desire for a kiss might actually prompt us to some pretty impulsive behavior. Even to a point of craziness where we might not recognize ourselves (but our girlfriends might know all too well!).

Yet kissing remains the purest, simplest form of expression. Like love, happiness, desire, tenderness, even outright lust. It's that special way to bond with your significant other (or "Mr. Right" right now), be it at the door at the end of the day, on the pillow first thing in the morning or anywhere else the mood moves you.

Kissing also has the ability to do marvelous things, like soothe you from a crazy day, free you from some emotional baggage, rekindle those magical emotions and make your hubba-hubba ding-ding for other feel-good sexy pleasures. It's a private, intimate, "two souls as one" vibe that for some is more significant and intense than sex.

survey says...

When asked which they'd give up if they had to—kissing or sex—a resounding 63 percent said sex. Many believe kissing will outlive sex. And while they could survive without sex, they couldn't survive without kissing. Some declared they'd give up food before forgoing kissing! Twenty-one percent would give up kissing, and 16 percent thought it was too hard a question to answer.

The wonderful thing, on top of all this, is that kissing is also downright good for you. Just ask a doctor. A kiss a day will keep them away. Luscious lip-locking can leave you rested, rosy and glowing like you've been pampered. So you should make every effort to kiss as much and as often as you can. It could be the priceless panacea for a multitude of things that may ail you.

did you know ?

The act of kissing can produce the same hormone in your body that firing a gun does. Dyn-'O-Mite! That's some firecrackin', star-spangled explosion!

kissing: it does a body and soul good

"A kiss makes the heart young again and
wipes out the years."

RUPERT BROOKE

Appreciating how wonderful kissing feels, it also offers real tangible health benefits that can make you feel wonderful. A nice smooch does all sorts of amazing things for our bodies, our quality of life, and maybe even our pocketbooks.

PHYSICAL & EMOTIONAL EFFECTS

Medical experts say passionate puckering is a natural way to:

- *Prevent Cavities and Tooth Decay*: Kissing is our own internal dental hygiene system. When we swap spit, we create more saliva in our mouths. And that washes away plaque. Next time your dentist says, "Ah, I see you've been brushing and flossing," tell them yes, but it's really kissing that's made for your beautiful teeth and gums!

- *Reduce Stress and Anxiety*: Kissing is the body's way to relieve tension. Forget the contortions of yoga, monotonous meditation tapes and those expensive prescription medications. When you're smooching, your mouth is literally almost smiling. You're breathing deeper. And your eyes are pretty much closed. All relaxing Zen movements. Kissing not only mellows your spirit, it lowers your blood pressure, too.

- *Protect Against Illness*: Kissing boosts oxytocin and other chemicals in the body that help fight off disease. It boosts your immune system, too. When you're making-out, you're sharing germs, which adds to your own internal defense mechanism. It's the best way to get some "good for you" bacteria!

did you know ?

During a kiss, a whopping 278 colonies of bacteria are exchanged. That could give anyone the heebie-jeebies when you stop to think about it!

- *Plump Your Lips*: Everyone wants puffier, poutier, sexier lips. Forget expensive collagen injections. Just smooch a lot. Regular, active kissing leaves your lips slightly swollen and naturally pink. Your friends will be wondering what kind of lipstick you're using.
- *Make You Look Younger*: Kissing can even slow the aging process. It tones the jaw and cheek muscles, which can reduce saggy chicken neck (honest). And French kissing is the most effective way to tighten the underlying face muscles. All that tongue tangoing requires the flexing of thirty-four facial muscles!

- *Improve Fitness*: Playing tonsil hockey is a great workout. It's a heart-pumping/pulse-racing exercise that doesn't require a pricey gym membership. And when you get into real serious smooching, you're using all sorts of muscles and tendons for total body conditioning. People will notice you're lookin' mighty fine. Good enough to kiss, even!

- *Lose Weight*: A night of juicy smacks can increase your metabolism. Depending on the intensity of your passion, you can kiss away two to six calories a minute (as compared to eleven calories on a treadmill). That's got to be the nicest way to eliminate dessert before it reaches your hips!

- *Boost Self-Esteem*: Forget shopping. Kissing is one of the best ways to improve your state of mind. The intimacy of a canoodling with someone special makes you feel good. And when you feel happy, you feel good about yourself.

- *Improves Your Skin*: Scientific tests have shown kissing can even help reduce skin problems. Your skin will shimmer like sequins, so get smooching!

KISSING MIGHT EVEN . . .

And if that doesn't give you enough incentive, kissing just might:

- *Reduce PMS.* Gentle, sweet smooching around that "special time" could possibly alleviate symptoms like cramping and irritability. At the very least, it will certainly get your mind off of it!

- *Save Money.* Kissing will occupy your time in a productive way. It will reduce your need to shop for another "to die for" pair of shoes you really don't need, go out partying for the tenth night in a row, and keep you away from ordering all those handy whats-a-ma-hoosies from late-night infomercials.

- *Increase Your Allure Factor.* Kissing gives you that fresh, head-turning look. Between those curvaceous, rosy lips, smiling face and certain twinkle, you'll receive many a compliment.

more views
on kissing

"I was born when you kissed me. I died when you left me.

I lived a few days when you loved me."

HUMPHREY BOGART TO GLORIA GRAHAME

(*IN A LONELY PLACE*, 1950)

The ladies of the *Kissing* survey had more to chat about on the subject of kissing. As always, they had lovely, wise things to share.

WHAT IS THE IMPORTANCE OF KISSING IN YOUR ROMANTIC LIFE?

"My husband loves to kiss . . . it is an especially

important part of foreplay for him."

T. W.

"It's the thing that gives you that rumble in your stomach
unlike anything else. It's erotic and sexy. Can be the
best fun with your clothes on. Remember, kissing
doesn't have to always be lips to lips . . . there's
lips to cheek, ears, neck . . . you get the picture."

M . T .

"Hugely important to make a connection when out in
public, and when in private, it signifies the souls coming
together (it is sort of beyond sex)."

A . S .

"I think it is the purest, most endearing form
of love and romance."

A . M .

"It conveys affection and let's my husband know I'm
thinking about him in a tender way. It's a way to
show emotion—happy, flirty, passionate, desirous,
fun, teasing, serious, etc."

L . R .

DO YOU CONSIDER KISSING CHEATING?

This is a tricky subject. We've all wondered how we'd react if the sugarplum in our life were to kiss someone else. Or what we might do if tempted.

A resounding 66 percent of the ladies believe kissing is cheating—*if you've kissed, you've cheated in your mind and with your lips.*

However, true to the beautifully complex nature of the female mind, some of these same women wished kissing wasn't considered cheating if it was them doing the kissing. But if their significant other was to kiss some hoochie, you bet it's cheating.

"Sometimes a kiss is just a kiss. No harm. No foul."

S . W .

"It depends on how long the kiss lasts and who you're kissing. A kiss without passion is not cheating. A smooch hello is not cheating."

N . C .

WHAT CRAZY THINGS HAVE YOU DONE IN THE NAME OF A KISS?

"I basically grabbed a guy I adored and
forced my kiss on him!!"

H . J .

"I once kissed a man I had just met at a cocktail party, in
the hallway of the party . . . we just couldn't help it—
it was a total chemistry thing."

B . P .

"Left a note for someone to meet me
in a remote place."

P . K .

"I used to be something of a band groupie.
I kissed a fair number of lead singers, guitarists
and drummers, and I have a drumstick and
pick collection to prove it . . ."

E . H .

"Drove in a car for two hours just to reunite with someone I had a fling with. It was not worth the trip!"

G . V .

"Begged for one."

V . W .

"Met up with an old flame at a party and ducked
into the stairway of the building to neck
uncontrollably like schoolkids."

D . M .

"I wore the same costume as the head cheerleader to the
high school masquerade party in order to steal a kiss from
her boyfriend, the cutest guy in school."

B . F .

"Danced on a bar and played strip poker."

N . C .

It's good to be moved slightly out of our comfort zone
for a kiss. Life would be a tad on the dull side if the crav-

ing for one didn't provoke some frisky behavior once in a while.

VALENTINE'S DAY SPECIALS

- February 14th, 269 A.D.: The first St. Valentine's Day. According to Roman legend, a man named Valentinus was sentenced to death for his Christian beliefs. While in jail, Valentinus restored the sight of his jailer's blind daughter (nice guy, considering!). The night before he died, he wrote a farewell note to the girl, signed, "From Your Valentine." His sentence was carried out the next day, February 14th.

- Fifth century: Romans honored Juno, the pagan goddess of love and marriage, on February 14th. During the celebration, guys would draw girls' names and court them for marriage (more like a lottery!). At the end of the century (498), Pope Gelasius declared the day as St. Valentine's Day to honor the martyr Valentinus, and ended the pagan celebration.

- 1477: The earliest known Valentine is written by Margery Brews of England to her "right worshipful and well-beloved Valentine." She hopes he'll make her the "merriest maiden on the ground and marry her despite her meager dowry."

- 1910: Hallmark is established by J. C. Hall, who arrived in Kansas City with a shoebox filled with postcards to sell. Hallmark sold its first Valentine's Day card in 1913. Today, approximately 74 million romantics celebrate the holiday. And 65 percent of them give Valentine's Day cards. Good thing Hallmark has nearly 1,500 different ones to choose from!

♡

daily kisses xoxo

1. Every kiss with your sweetheart should be as romantic as a Valentine's Day kiss.

2. Make kissing part of your weekly regimen. Just as it's recommended to work out three times a week for thirty minutes, try to get in a few hot 'n heavy make-out sessions, too!

3. Be it a kiss of sweet love, tender romance or just because, to give is as good as to receive. It will leave you smiling and feeling happy, too!

11
a few parting words of kissing advice

"The slowest kiss makes too much haste."

THOMAS MIDDLETON

(*A CHASTE MAIDEN IN SEASIDE*, 1613)

Our lovely lady friends and chivalrous guy friends of the *Kissing* survey wanted to send us off with some of their own personal bits to ponder. They have much good kissing wisdom to share!

girl-to-girl advice

"As great as it is, don't just give it away. Maybe that's
why it's great. Kissing isn't for just anyone. Pick your
man carefully. How disappointing if it's bad. How
great when it's great. Discrimination is the key."

L . J .

"Take your time . . . no need to rush. Slow is nice, but
don't let the other person do all the work; that's no fun!
Be creative and have fun with it!"

N . S .

"Make it fun! It was fun when we invented numbers to go
with our kisses—although we can never remember which
number is which kiss, but it makes us giggle . . ."

S . L .

"Hold back just a bit before the contact,
then light touch for first kiss."

P . K .

"Let loose and get your groove on."

P . L .

"Not too sloppy, not too dry. Never known a guy not to
love having his lips gently nipped with my teeth."

E . H .

"Enjoy it every time. I'd like to add that we should
stop to enjoy kisses of all kinds, too . . . from the
most innocent kiss of a gleeful child, to the
comforting kiss of a parent, to the intoxicating kiss
of someone special. . . . It's not advice on technique,
but in my humble opinion, this advice will last longer."

M . L .

"Do it more often; it brings people closer
together more than they think."

L . T .

"Do it with the right partner."

F . S .

"The more, the merrier."

B . N .

"No licking."

C . M .

"Let it carry/transport you. Don't work too hard at it.
Let it just happen."

C . R .

"Take it slow. If you want to learn how to do it better, let
him guide, and see where it takes you. Or be playful with
it. Flirt while you kiss, pull away for a second and give him
a really sultry look. It will draw him right back in."

C . L .

"Don't be afraid to make the first move.
Always ask yourself, 'If I kiss this guy, am I
going to regret it in the morning?' "

M . V .

guy-to-girl advice

"Relax and let things flow. Let the passion build and revel
in the sensuality of the moment."

E . H .

"Confidence. Approach when it's not expected—
like on an elevator or in a restaurant on the way
back from the bathroom."

S . D .

"Don't be shy about nibbling, be it the lips,
ears, chest or nipples."

C . C .

"Kissing is the best thing about a relationship, and everything should be done to sustain that. Girls should be adventurous in their kissing—there's no right or wrong, as
long as you both want the same thing. . . ."

C . E .

"The more aggressive, the better. I know guys are one-dimensional, but aggressive initial action leads to better action down the road. If they want to make a guy weak in the knees, the more forceful, the better."

A . M .

"It's all about her body language."

Y . D .

"Just make it passionate and plentiful. Kissing is best done with quality and quantity!"

N . K .

"Whisper in his ear. It doesn't have to be dirty, just intimate."

J . D .

♡

12
the *kissing* survey

When it comes to kissing, after actually doing it, what does a girl love more than to think about it and then talk about it with her girlfriends? To revel in and relive those sweet 'n sexy, special, romantic kisses, here's the *Kissing* survey and some extra fun.

Do it on your own or with your friends. Enjoy reminiscing about those memorable kisses, be they good or not so good.

There's even an extra bonus section that will show you how to take a closer look at the boys you've been kissing, in a way that might tell you a little something about yourself you might not have otherwise known.

take the survey

1. What's your definition of a kiss? How does it make you feel?

2. How often do you kiss romantically?
    a. Daily
    b. Weekly
    c. Monthly
    d. Not enough
    e. Any chance you get

3. How do you rate yourself as a kisser?
    a. Red hot, if you do say so yourself
    b. Pretty good but open to suggestions
    c. Short on technique yet enthusiastic
    d. Other_____

4. Describe your:
    • First kiss (how old, what happened, how you felt, etc.)

- Most memorable/special kiss
- Most embarrassing or unusual kiss
- Scandalous, most outrageous kiss

5. Do you kiss with your eyes:
    a. Open
    b. Closed
    c. A combination of both

6. What do you think makes a great kiss?

7. What part of your body do you like to be kissed on? Where's your "goose bump" zone?

8. How would you rather spend an afternoon:
    a. Shopping for hot shoes on sale
    b. Kissing languorously on a couch
    c. Getting a manicure/pedicure
    d. Getting a massage

9. What puts you in the mood to kiss? What breaks the mood?

10. When you're in the mood to kiss, do you:
    a. Make the first move
    b. Let someone else make the first move
    c. Play it by ear

11. If your honey is in the mood to kiss, but you're not, do you:
    a. Push him away
    b. Give him a little peck
    c. Act like a good sport and try to get into it
    d. You're never *not* in the mood to kiss

12. Where do you like to kiss? Where have you enjoyed some juicy canoodling?

13. What movies have the best/most memorable kissing scenes?

14. What's sexier, kissing a guy who:
    a. Looks like a movie star but is totally full of himself

    b. Has a great sense of humor

    c. Has a hot car and money

    d. Is a geek but totally sweet

15. What person(s), famous or otherwise, would you want to be stranded with on a desert island, knowing kissing would be the best way to past the time?

16. Do you consider kissing cheating?

    a. Yes

    b. No

    c. It depends (explain)

17. Have you ever kissed a friend's boyfriend/significant other?

    a. Yes

    b. No

    c. Came close

18. What would you do if your significant other kissed someone else?

    a. Break up with him

b. Forgive him

c. Kiss someone else for revenge

19. If you had to give up kissing or sex, which would it be?

a. Kissing

b. Sex

20. What best describes your attitude toward a kiss when it comes to chemistry and satisfaction?

a. If you kiss a guy and he's not such a great kisser, you think with a little practice he can become a better kisser

b. If you kiss a guy and he's not such a great kisser, all physical attraction ends for you right there

c. If you kiss a guy and he's not such a great kisser, you look past the kissing and focus on other positive qualities

what's your kissing profile?

Have you ever wondered what your kissing tells you about yourself? Well, here's a little way to take a look at what's going on with your kissing.

It's can be very helpful for girls who are dating a lot, as it might shed light on the type of guy they're attracted to. For happily married ladies, use this to take a walk down memory lane—what do the details of the boys you've kissed in the past say about the boy you're kissing now?

HERE'S HOW:

1. Write down the first names or initials of all the boys you can remember kissing.
2. Next to their name/initials, write down:
    a. The color of their hair and eyes
    b. Their height—tall, medium, on the shorter side, etc.

    c. Any other physical characteristics you want to make note of, e.g., if they're athletic, a couch potato, etc.

3. Write down their personality, e.g., quiet, comedian, intellectual, creative, etc. You can also make note of things like what they do for a living, what kind of car they drive, how they dress, etc., anything you want to note.

4. Ask yourself who made the first move—you or him?

5. Rate the kissing on a scale of 1–5, with 1 being a "dead on arrival" and 5 being a knee-melter.

Now, take a look at this mini kissing report. Do you notice any patterns? Like, do the guys you've kissed tend to have brown hair and light eyes? Are you attracted to the strong, silent type? Do you wait for them to make the move? Or are you the bold one? You might find yourself saying, "Ah, very interesting . . . Who knew?"

Use this Kissing report as a game plan to find that certain someone who's just right for you. Or keep it as diary of your kissing escapades to reminisce and enjoy anytime!

♡

more reading on kissing

If you are interested in learning more about kissing, check out the following resources for information and inspiration.

books

Anatomy of Love by Helen E. Fisher, Ph.D. New York: Fawcett Books, 1992.

The Art of Kissing by William Cane. New York: St. Martin's Griffin, 1994.

The Kama Sutra of Vatsyana Translated from the Sanskrit Text by the Hindoo Kama Shastra Society Printed for the Society of Friends to India Benares—New York, 1883.

"The Book of Kisses" edited by William Cane. New York: St. Martin's Press, 1993.

websites

www.flirt.com

www.links2love.com

www.futzai.com

www.nzgirl.com

www.redhotkissingtips.com

www.kissingbooth.com

www.romancetuck.com

www.kissingnet.com

www.singlescafe.com

www.my.webmd.com

acknowledgments

Many thanks to:

Vaughn M. Bryant, Ph.D. (Texas A&M University)

Helen E. Fisher, Ph.D. (Rutgers University)

Billie Fitzpatrick

Lewis Frumkes

Carla Glasser

Henry E. Higgins

David Hirshey

Marian Lizzi

Kirsten Manges

Kim Schefler

Jane von Mehren

All the respondents who participated
in the *Kissing* survey

Lifelong girlfriends, boyfriends and cheerleaders

And my Pops for his love and kisses

x ♡ o

about the author

Andréa Demirjian is an independent marketing and advertising consultant who's had a lifelong passion for kissing and all things kissable. A former advertising agency executive and a native New Yorker, she lives in Manhattan and Quogue, New York. This is her first book.

www.kissingbook.com